THE REMINISCENCES OF
Master Chief Boatswain's Mate Carl M. Brashear U.S. Navy (Retired)

INTERVIEWED BY
Paul Stillwell

U.S. Naval Institute • Annapolis, Maryland

Copyright © 1998

Preface

To become the first black master diver in the Navy, Carl Brashear used a rare combination of grit, determination, and persistence, because the obstacles in his path were formidable. His race was a handicap, as were his origin on a sharecropper's farm in rural Kentucky and the modest amount of education he received there. But these were not his greatest challenges. He was held back by an even bigger factor: in 1966 his left leg was amputated just below the knee because he was badly injured on a salvage operation.

After the amputation, the Navy sought to retire Brashear from active duty, but he refused to submit to the decision. Instead, he secretly returned to diving and produced evidence that he could still excel, despite his injury. Then, in 1970, he qualified as a master diver, a difficult feat under any circumstances and something no black man had accomplished before. By the time of his retirement, he had achieved the highest possible rate for Navy enlisted personnel, master chief petty officer. In addition, he had become a celebrity through his response to manifold challenges and thereby had become a real inspiration to others.

This oral history covers a number of topics, including Navy racism, diving and salvage operations, officer-enlisted relations on board ship, the recovery of a nuclear weapon that fell into the sea near Spain, and the Navy's efforts to combat alcoholism. Master Chief Brashear is painfully candid in discussing the successful treatment he received while going through the Navy's alcohol rehabilitation program.

Carl Brashear's composite portrait is of an individual motivated by a thirst for excitement and adventure. He found it in the Navy, and he found himself driven by a motivation to excel. He prided himself on looking sharp and doing his job well. His remedy for the obstacles he faced was hard work. His story is an example of what an individual can achieve when he is determined to meet his goals.

In moving from the raw transcript to this finished form, both Master Chief Brashear and I have done some editing. I have added annotating footnotes to explain terms and provide additional information for readers.

Ms. Ann Hassinger of the Naval Institute's history division has made a significant contribution through her diligence in the overall process of printing, proofreading, and overseeing the binding of the completed volumes.

                                                Paul Stillwell
                                                Director, History Division
                                                U.S. Naval Institute
                                                February 1998

MASTER CHIEF BOATSWAIN'S MATE CARL MAXIE BRASHEAR
UNITED STATES NAVY (RETIRED)

Personal Data

Born: January 19, 1931, Tonieville, Larue County, Kentucky
Parents: McDonald and Gonzella Brashear
Married: Junetta Wilcoxson in 1952; divorced in 1978
    Hattie R. Elam in 1980; divorced in 1983
    Jeanette A. Brundage in 1985; divorced in 1987
Children: Shazanta Brashear, born on May 17, 1955; died 13 July 1996
    DaWayne Brashear, born on January 16, 1957
    Phillip M. Brashear, born on July 4, 1962
    Patrick S. Brashear, born on July 31, 1964
Education: Sonora Grade School, Sonora, Kentucky, 1937-46
    Passed GED test in U.S. Navy, 1960
    Charles County Community College, Great Mills, Maryland, 1980-82
    Tidewater Community College, Virginia Beach, Virginia, 1983

Dates of Rates

Seaman Recruit (E-1) through Boatswain's Mate First Class (E-6), 1948-55
Chief Boatswain's Mate (E-7), 1960-66
Senior Chief Boatswain's Mate (E-8), 1966-71
Master Chief Boatswain's Mate (E-9), 1971-79

Dates of Diving Specialties

Salvage Diver, 1953-60
Second Class Diver, 1960-64
First Class Diver, 1964-70
Saturation Diver, 1970-79
Master Diver, 1970-79

Decorations and Medals

Good Conduct Medal (eight awards)
Navy Commendation Medal
Navy Achievement Medal
National Defense Service Medal
China Service Medal
Korean Service Medal

United Nations Medal
Navy and Marine Corps Medal
Armed Forces Expeditionary Medal
Presidential Unit Citation
Navy Occupation Service Medal

Chronological Transcript of Service

February 25, 1948: Enlisted in the U.S. Navy

February-May 1948: Naval Training Center, Great Lakes, Illinois--Recruit Training

May 1948-June 1950: Squadron VX-1, Key West, Florida--Officers' Mess; PBM Beachmaster Unit

June 1950-November 1951: USS Palau (CVE-122)--Deck Division; Motor Whaleboat Coxswain

November 1951-March 1955: USS Tripoli (CVE-64)--Second Division Petty Officer; Master-at-Arms; Temporary Additional Duty at Salvage Diving School

March 1955-June 1956: USS Opportune (ARS-41)--Deck Division; Salvage Diver; Section Leader; Repair Party Leader

June 1956-June 1958: Naval Air Station, Quonset Point, Rhode Island--Leading Petty Officer; Salvage Diver; Escort for President Dwight D. Eisenhower

June 1958-July 1960: Ship Repair Facility, Guam, Marianas Islands--Salvage Diver; Skipper of Yard Salvage Derrick

July-September 1960: Deep-Sea Diving School, Washington, D.C.--Student, failed the course

September 1960-March 1961: USS Nereus (AS-17)--Deck Division Chief Boatswain's Mate

March 1961-April 1962: Fleet Training Center, Pearl Harbor, Hawaii--Chief Master-at-Arms; Requalified as Second Class Diver; Temporary Additional Duty with Joint Task Force Eight

April 1962-October 1963: USS Coucal (ASR-8)--Ship's Chief Boatswain's Mate; Second Class Diver; Underway Officer of the Deck; In-Port Duty Chief

October 1963-June 1964: Deep-Sea Diving School, Washington, D.C.--Student, graduated as First Class Diver

June 1964-September 1965: USS Shakori (ATF-162)--Ship's Chief Boatswain's Mate; Leading Diver; Underway Officer of the Deck

September 1965-March 1966: USS Hoist (ARS-40)--Ship's Chief Boatswain's Mate; Acting Master Diver; Underway Officer of the Deck; Repair Party Leader; In-Port Duty Chief

May 1966-March 1967: Naval Regional Medical Center, Portsmouth, Virginia--Treatment following the amputation of left leg below the knee

March 1967-March 1968: Harbor Clearance Unit Two--Under Evaluation at Diving School for return to full active duty and diving

March 1968-December 1969: Naval Air Station, Norfolk, Virginia--Leading Chief Petty Officer; Leading Diver

December 1969-June 1970: Experimental Diving Unit, Deep-Sea Diving School, Washington, D.C.--Saturation Diver; Master Diver Evaluation

June 1970-May 1971: USS Hunley (AS-31)--Master Diver; R-7 Division Officer; In-Port Officer of the Deck; Minority Affairs Officer

May 1971-June 1975: USS Recovery (ARS-43)--Master Diver; Work Center Supervisor; Command Master Chief; Repair Party Leader; Underway Officer of the Deck; In-Port Command Duty Officer

June 1975-June 1977: Naval Safety Center, Norfolk, Virginia--Master Diver

June 1977-October 1978: USS Recovery (ARS-43)--Master Diver; Work Center Supervisor; Command Master Chief; Enlisted Watch Officer; Repair Party Leader; Underway Officer of the Deck; In-Port Command Duty Officer

October 1978-March 1979: Shore Intermediate Maintenance Activity, Norfolk, Virginia--Master Diver

April 1, 1979: Retired from the U.S. Navy as a master chief petty officer and master diver

Civilian Employment

April 1979-August 1980: QED Systems, Inc., Virginia Beach, Virginia--Diving Study for the Royal Saudi Navy; USS Forrestal (CV-59) Service Life Extension Program

February-November 1982: CDI Marine Company, Chesapeake, Virginia--Engineering Technician

November 1982-January 1993: Naval Communication Area Master Station Atlantic, Norfolk, Virginia--Environmental Protection Specialist; Energy Conservation Specialist

January 1993: Retired from government service in the grade of GS-11

Authorization

The U.S. Naval Institute is hereby authorized to make available to individuals, libraries, and other repositories of its choosing the transcripts of two oral history interviews concerning the life and career of the undersigned. The interviews were recorded on 17 November 1989 and 2 March 1990 in collaboration with Paul Stillwell for the U.S. Naval Institute.

The literary rights to the interviews will be the joint property of Carl Brashear and the U.S. Naval Institute. The copyright in both the oral and transcribed versions shall be held jointly by Carl Brashear and the U.S. Naval Institute. The tape recordings of the interviews are and will remain the property of the U.S. Naval Institute.

Signed and sealed this __20__ day of __JUNE__ 1996.

_____
BMCM Carl M. Brashear, U.S. Navy (Retired)

_____
Paul Stillwell for the U.S. Naval Institute

Interview Number 1 with Master Chief Boatswain's Mate Carl M. Brashear, U.S. Navy (Retired)

Place: U.S. Naval Station, Norfolk, Virginia

Date: Friday, 17 November 1989

Interviewer: Paul Stillwell

Q: Master Chief, just to begin at the beginning, could you please tell me when and where you were born and what you remember of your early childhood?

Master Chief Brashear: Yes, Stillwell, I was born in Tonieville, Kentucky, in January 1931. That was in Larue County. When I was about six weeks old, we moved to a farm that was about three miles out of a little town called Sonora in Hardin County, Kentucky. There my father was a sharecropper for a Dr. Glasscock and his wife.* I lived on the farm until age 17. During my early childhood, I attended school in a one-room schoolhouse.

Q: Segregated, I presume.

Master Chief Brashear: Yes, a segregated schoolhouse with broken-out windows and hand-me-down books. I attended that school from the first to the eighth grade.

Q: Would you, in retrospect, comment on the quality of that education?

Master Chief Brashear: Well, the quality of the education was satisfactory. Then my mother would take up the slack on things we didn't get in school. She sort of taught a home course in reading, writing, and math. But the school itself was satisfactory.

---

* A sharecropper is a tenant farmer whom the landlord provides credit for seed, tools, living quarters, and food. The tenant works the land and receives an agreed share of the crop's value, minus the credits previously advanced.

Q: How much education did your parents have?

Master Chief Brashear: My mother went through the ninth grade, and my father had a third-grade education.

Q: I'm sure you learned a lot about hard work at that farm too.

Master Chief Brashear: Yes. We all had our chores to do on the farm, Stillwell. I'd get up before daylight in the morning. Once I became of age, I milked three or four cows, chopped wood, and did chores like that. Then I walked three miles to school. We went to school in the rain, snow, sleet or what have you. Then, when we got to the schoolhouse, we had to build fire in a pot-bellied stove. It would be around 9:00 o'clock before the schoolhouse got warm enough for us to start our classes. That's the situation that was there then.

Q: One advantage during the Depression, at least in the sharecropping situation, was that your parents would have steady employment.[*]

Master Chief Brashear: Yes, he was steady employed, and we always had plenty of food because we raised everything on the farm. As a matter of fact, we had enough food on the farm to feed the whole community. I recall on weekends, Saturdays and Sundays, my mother and father would hook up a wagon, and they would distribute food around in the neighborhood. This went on for some time.

Q: What did you have in the way of brothers and sisters?

---

[*] Following the crash of the New York Stock Exchange in late October 1929, the United States was plunged into the Great Depression, from which it did not recover until the nation geared up for World War II at the beginning of the 1940s. The Depression was marked by high unemployment and many business failures.

Master Chief Brashear: Including my father and mother, there were nine of us in the family. I'm number six. We lost a sister when she was about six weeks old. The rest of my brothers and sisters are still living. My father passed away in 1974.

We lived on the farm, Stillwell. We didn't know much about it. We thought that was a good way to live. We didn't have electricity, didn't have running water, but we were happy. We had a lot of love in our family, a lot of togetherness. The entertainment in the evening was my father telling jokes and playing with us and things of this nature.

Q: Did you go hunting with him?

Master Chief Brashear: Many times. We'd go hunting, and we had about every kind of gun, I guess it was, in the house. We had rifles and shotguns and pistols, and we would go rabbit hunting and squirrels, doves, quails. Any kind of game that's in Kentucky, that's what we hunted.

Q: Those are very important times for father and son together.

Master Chief Brashear: Very important. And, of course, we fished a lot. A lot of times, we'd go fishing on Sunday mornings. Before everybody went to church, we'd go fishing and catch us a couple of fish. There was just a lot of togetherness.

Q: How big a part did religion play in the family life?

Master Chief Brashear: I think our faith was what kept us going. Well, it played a big part. My great-uncle was a preacher, and there were a lot of deacons and preachers throughout the family.

Q: What denomination was that?

Master Chief Brashear: Southern Baptist, I guess you would call it, or just Baptist.

Q: Was Sunday completely a day of rest?

Master Chief Brashear: Sunday was completely a day of rest. Nothing happened on the farm on Sunday. As a matter of fact, my father would knock off work on Saturday at noon, and then he'd go to town and assist my mother and everybody in doing the shopping, what little bit we had to buy in town. So, actually, we knocked off work at Saturday noon. But the rest of the time, from sunup to sundown, we worked on the farm. And all of that cultivating of the crops was done with horses and mules--no tractors, nothing like that.

Q: When did you first encounter prejudice?

Master Chief Brashear: When I was about five or six years old. When we would be walking to school in the sleet and the mud and snow, the white kids would be riding the bus. That's when I realized what was going on. Of course, there were no movies in the little community that I lived in, but we would go to Elizabethtown, which is about 11 miles from where we lived, to see a movie or something like that. When we did, we'd have to go in the back of the bus. This was when I realized that there was prejudice.

Q: And apparently that segregation was a situation that was accepted by both sides?

Master Chief Brashear: Oh, yes. It certainly was. We didn't know any different. We thought this was the way of life, and we just accepted it. Now, of course, in the little community that I lived in we didn't feel it as much as once we went to a larger city. Because in the little community we lived in, everybody knew each other, with the exception that we went to separate schools.

Q: Did you have friends in the white community?

Master Chief Brashear: Oh, yes. We had a lot of friends in the white community. They would come to our house and help sharecrop, and we'd all be around the same table. Or we'd go to their houses, or their places, and sharecrop. They called it swap working on the farm. We would all be in the same area--eating, laughing, and talking. If we had to stay at somebody's house, a lot of times they would sleep in the same bed. So we didn't feel the brunt of the prejudice in my community.

Q: Probably at that time some of the former slaves were still around. Do you remember meeting and hearing them?

Master Chief Brashear: No, I don't recall meeting any of the slaves.

Q: Did you set goals for yourself in that period? What did you hope to be?

Master Chief Brashear: Stillwell, I didn't set any goals for myself during that period. But looking back on my life now, I always was doing things that were exciting, daring things. I recall when I was 13 years old, and this guy had a 74 Harley-Davidson motorcycle. Well, he needed a part for a car, so I rode the motorcycle 11 miles over to Elizabethtown to get it. Well, my mother found out about this. She ran down to the little station where you crank up one of those telephones to try to get the policemen to stop me on that motorcycle. But before she could get a telephone call through to the next town, I had been to the Western Auto, picked up the part, and on the way back, riding a big 74 Harley-Davidson motorcycle. I was 13 years old.

Q: What other things did you do like that?

Master Chief Brashear: Well, we had a creek called the Glendale Creek. I used to swim across that creek. I used to cut church on Sundays and swim certain distances. Gee, I was just a young kid when I went swimming in those lakes. That was a pretty daring thing to do. One time my father gave me a horse and a saddle, and I'd have that horse doing things. I'd take him uptown, and he'd stand way up, you know. Then I had rope where I could rope a cow and things like that. I was always doing daring things.

Q: You were going to be a cowboy.

Master Chief Brashear: Well, I didn't know really what I wanted to be, but I just wanted to do things that were exciting. As far as a goal, though, I didn't have one during those days.

Q: How much reading did you do on your own?

Master Chief Brashear: Quite a bit. We would have to do a certain amount of reading and understanding what we read for my mom.

Q: What kinds of things did you read?

Master Chief Brashear: Well, we would read the funny paper and magazines, and my mother had this <u>Home Life</u> magazine we used to read quite a bit, because this was about the only thing that we could buy. Then the rest were just newspapers and magazines that came down from the people that we were sharecroppers for.

Q: Did you have a radio?

Master Chief Brashear: We didn't have a radio until around 1939 or 1940. We got our first radio, and it was the kind you would have to run off of a battery.

Q: I'm sure that was a big event.

Master Chief Brashear: That was a big event in our lives, to get a radio. I remember the first time that we listened to a fight with Joe Louis, we had that radio.* Other times we used to go up to the people's house that we sharecropped for, when we'd want to listen to some big event on the radio. But we did have what we called in those days a Victrola, one of those things you wound up, and it played records. We used to entertain ourselves dancing with our sisters.

Q: How soon did you get your first real girlfriend?

Master Chief Brashear: Well, I didn't get a real girlfriend until I was around 15 or 16, and that girl was living in the next town. Elizabethtown was the next largest city that we would go to, and that's where she lived. I was around 15 or 16.

Q: How good a student were you in school?

Master Chief Brashear: Well, according to the teacher when I went back to Kentucky, when they had the Carl Brashear day there not too long ago, she said I didn't have to study and I'd make A's and B's.

Q: Great!

Master Chief Brashear: So I was a very good student, but I didn't like school. I really didn't like school.

Q: Why not?

---

* Joseph Louis Barrow (1914-1981) was a black boxer who fought under the name Joe Louis. He won the heavyweight championship in 1936 and successfully defended the title 25 times before retiring in 1949. A later comeback failed.

Master Chief Brashear: Well, I guess I was just like the average kid. I thought I could do things without an education. I didn't attend high school before I joined the Navy.

Q: I see.

By the time World War II came, I guess you were too young to take part in that.

Master Chief Brashear: Yes, I was too young, but I remember World War II. In 1941 I thought that the people were going to come over and kill us. I was very frightened, very scared when my father told us that we were in the war. We would also read in the papers what was going on and would hear it from the people that we were sharecropping from.

Q: By the time you got to your late teens, did you have a better idea of what you wanted to do with your life?

Master Chief Brashear: Yes. My brother-in-law was a soldier, and so at a very early age, I'd say around 14, I wanted to be a soldier or a military man. When I was 17, I went to enlist in the Army. The Army people were screaming and yelling at me. They had me so scared I didn't know what I was doing, and I failed the entrance exam for the Army. I was supposed to go back and take it in the next couple of days, but instead I joined the Navy.

Q: Why did you make that switch?

Master Chief Brashear: Well, when I came back from Fort Knox, I stopped in Elizabethtown. I saw the Navy recruiting office and stopped in to talk to the recruiter. The chief treated me so nice, and I told him what I had done, that I'd been to Fort Knox.

He said, "Well, let me talk to you about the Navy."

So he discussed with me at length that the Navy would treat me nice.

So I said, "Well, I'm not going back. I'll enlist in the Navy."

Q: It's interesting that one person can make that much difference in your life.

Master Chief Brashear: Yes. He didn't scream at me like the one at Fort Knox. Also, they had me in a very cold barracks where I was supposed to take an exam, set aside from other people, and I just failed the exam.

Q: What year was that?

Master Chief Brashear: That was in 1948.

Q: That was the year that the services were officially integrated.*

Master Chief Brashear: Yes, 1948. So I joined the Navy and never went back to enlist in the Army. Looking back now, I think I was better off, anyway, by coming into the Navy, although I did join the Navy as a steward, and I worked as a steward about one year.

Q: Did you then go to boot camp?

Master Chief Brashear: Yes, I went to boot camp in February of '48 in Great Lakes, Illinois.† We were in an integrated company when I took my basic training there. From there I went to Key West, Florida.

Q: Great Lakes is cold place to be in February.

---

* On 26 July 1948, President Harry S Truman issued Executive Order 9981, which said, "It is hereby declared that there shall be equality of treatment and opportunity for all persons in the armed services without regard to race, color, religion, or national origin."
† The naval training center at Great Lakes, north of Chicago on the shore of Lake Michigan, has long been one of the sites used by the Navy for recruit training.

Master Chief Brashear: Very cold: snow, sleeting, and raining. I made it through boot camp okay.

Q: What do you remember about the training?

Master Chief Brashear: Well, the training was very strict, and everything had to happen on time. They would sort of do things to you to try to get you angry or see how much you could take, just a lot of harassment during the training. But the training was very effective. I didn't much like the food when I first went to boot camp. But about four or five weeks into the boot camp, I was eating everything I could find. I stole a pie one day.

The chief petty officer came and saw me and said, "Son, you stole a pie, didn't you?"

I said, "Yep."

He said, "Was it good?"

I said, "Yes, sir."

He said, "Did you enjoy it?"

I said, "Yes, sir."

He said, "Well, that's fine." He said, "Gee, we like to see people eat." He was talking to me just as nice as he could.

This was at noontime. And, man, I was telling all the kids I stole a pie and got away with it. At 4:00 o'clock, who'd I see standing in front of the barracks but the chief. He made me pull my watch cap down over my face, and then he had me walk in front of the Navy exchange, hitting on an empty pie pan with two spoons saying, "I stole a pie. I stole a pie." [Laughter] So I had to do that for two hours.

Q: That was a pretty effective lesson.

Master Chief Brashear: Yes, that was a good one. I never stole another pie. As a matter fact, I never stole anything else.

Q: Did you have any feelings of homesickness? This was a long way from what you'd been doing.

Master Chief Brashear: No. It was amazing. I didn't feel homesick. I didn't get that down feeling that some of the people in our company experienced. I didn't get that.

Q: Did you ever get any adverse treatment during your training because of being black?

Master Chief Brashear: No, I did not, not in basic training. They treated us all equal and all the same, it seemed to me. There wasn't any favoritism or anything like that. If there was, I didn't notice it. Grant and Churchill were our two company commanders. I can remember those two guys. Grant was a chief signalman and Churchill was a chief boatswain's mate.

Q: How much choice were you given in what you could be right after you got out of boot camp? Did you have any other choices besides steward?

Master Chief Brashear: Not immediately, no. I was assigned as a steward for squadron VX-1 at Key West, Florida.*

Q: What are your recollections of Key West?

Master Chief Brashear: Well, I didn't enjoy Key West too much. We were living on the seaplane base, and the only time that we could go swimming in the swimming pool was on Saturday mornings. That was from 9:00 o'clock until 12:00, one day a week. We lived in, of course, the stewards' barracks, and Key West was segregated. We had one street we could go to for liberty. Basically, that's about what we had to do in Key West, Florida.

But there is where I got out of the steward branch. I met Chief Boatswain's Mate Johnson, who used to work at Kinnock Ford here in Virginia Beach after he retired; he's

---

* VX-1--Experimental Squadron One.

still living.* I met Chief Johnson in sort of an unusual way. One day I went fishing over there where the Navy crews were beaching the seaplanes, and I watched them. I met Chief Johnson there, and he arranged for me to get out of the steward branch and come over to work for him as a beachmaster. There's where I got in a lot of swimming and a lot of training. That's where I developed, I think, a good love for the sea--from swimming out the side mounts to beach those seaplanes.

Q: Did you find that much more satisfying than the steward work?

Master Chief Brashear: Much more. And it was exciting, you know, swimming in the Gulf of Mexico beaching seaplanes. I'd get to swim from there over to the boathouse, and I enjoyed that much more. I really did feel more comfortable being in the United States Navy when I went from steward branch to the seaman branch and beaching those seaplanes.

Q: Where does this myth come from that blacks can't swim?

Master Chief Brashear: Well, I don't know where that came from. I recall we had a meeting in Washington, D.C., after I became a deep-sea diver--I may be getting ahead of myself--but there was a lot of talk about why blacks couldn't swim. One guy said it was due to the bone structure. One guy said they had too much negative buoyancy. But my theory is that blacks just weren't exposed to that environment. They weren't exposed to swimming pools, and this just wasn't in the black people's culture to swim. So this is the main reason that blacks don't swim. Blacks are not effective swimmers right now, on average. You never see a black guy swimming in the Olympics.

Q: So it's more a cultural thing, really.

Master Chief Brashear: Yes, it's more of a cultural problem.

---

* Master Chief Boatswain's Mate Guy P. Johnson, USN (Ret.)

Q: Were there any overt examples of discrimination and prejudice when you were out on liberty in Key West?

Master Chief Brashear: Well, we couldn't go to the nightclubs that the rest of the people went to. I recall one night we wanted to go into the Club Tropics, and they threw us out. But as far as getting along, we never had any violence.

Q: But you knew you had to stick pretty close to one area?

Master Chief Brashear: Yes.

Q: Can you talk more specifically about your duties involving the seaplanes? What kinds of planes were these?

Master Chief Brashear: Yes. VX-1 had two PBMs. Those were patrol bombers made by Martin. They were the type that you had to take the side mounts off before they got airborne. So when they would go off the ramp into the bay, we were required to disconnect the side mounts and then pull the side mounts back onto the beach. Of course, when the seaplane came back in and made up to the buoy, we would swim out with the tail hook and hook it on to the seaplane and bring it in close enough to the ramp. Then we'd have to swim out the side mounts and connect those up, and then we'd pull it on the beach.

Q: What were the side mounts?

Master Chief Brashear: The side mounts were the wheels, and they were mounted on a pontoon which floated. You hooked it up to a socket, and then you just twisted it under the seaplane. They'd bring up a connection like a ratchet, and it brought the fittings in under the seaplane.

Q: So then you could just wheel it ashore.

Master Chief Brashear: We had some D-8 Caterpillars, and we'd pull the planes onto the beach and then on into the hangar.

Q: How much chance did you have in that job to grow and learn and develop?

Master Chief Brashear: I think I grew up there and developed quite a bit in that assignment. I think I grew up quite a bit.

Q: What examples do you remember? What types of things did you learn?

Master Chief Brashear: Well, I learned how to get along with people, how to respect other people and to do my job without somebody coming around watching me quite a bit. I developed an attitude that, "I'm as smart as you are, and all I have to know is what you want me to do, and just let me do it." I didn't develop an attitude that people were picking on me or people were putting me in a different assignment. I just grew up, and I just developed a lot and had a good attitude there. I didn't have that type of attitude in the steward branch, because I didn't think I should be shining shoes and waiting on officers and doing just menial tasks. Even though I had an eighth-grade education, my GCT was 60.[*]

Q: Sounds as if Chief Johnson was an effective "sea daddy" for you.[†]

Master Chief Brashear: He was a "sea daddy."

---

[*] GCT--general classification test, a part of the battery of aptitude tests administered to Navy recruits.
[†] "Sea daddy" is slang term for an older person who takes a recruit or younger officer in hand and provides training and guidance on the individual's job.

Q: What kinds of things did he teach you?

Master Chief Brashear: He taught me basic seamanship up one side and down the other. He taught me how to be a good sailor, how to dress appropriately.

Q: What about leadership qualities? Did he work on those?

Master Chief Brashear: Yes, he did. He just worked on all phases of it. He developed a liking for me, and he would take me out to his house sometimes and just sit down and talk to me. He told me how to do things, how to adapt to various situations, and how to be a good sailor. That's the bottom line: to be a good man and a good sailor.

Q: There are a lot of things about shipboard seamanship that a boatswain's mate needs to know that you couldn't learn in the squadron. How did you pick up those things?

Master Chief Brashear: Well, when I went to my first ship, I had already advanced to third class boatswain's mate there in Key West. When I went to my first ship, which was the USS Palau, I was a good wire splicer.* You had to splice a lot of wire for the gear for those seaplanes, and we had to put in a lot of metallic sockets. The beach crew had a sewing machine in the beach house there, and I could sew well.

When I went to the Palau and reported in as a boatswain's mate, being the first time on a ship, well, I told my division petty officer what had happened. So he started me off in the sail locker--splicing wire, sewing, and what have you. I already knew how to use a boatswain's pipe, but I hadn't been on a ship to do it. I started off like that and putting in extra hours, learning the fuel rigs and the anchoring and mooring methods.

---

* The escort aircraft carrier Palau (CVE-122) was commissioned 19 February 1945. She had a displacement of 11,373 tons, was 557 feet long, 75 feet in the beam, an extreme width of 105 feet on the flight deck, and had a draft of 32 feet. She had a top speed of 19 knots and could accommodate approximately 33 aircraft.

Q: The things that boatswain's mates do.

Master Chief Brashear: The things that boatswain's mates do; that's right.

Q: Did you enjoy shipboard life?

Master Chief Brashear: I enjoyed shipboard life very much, but I didn't enjoy the USS Palau.

Q: Why not?

Master Chief Brashear: The USS Palau was my first sea assignment, and I wanted to be a diver. Well, when I put in a request to be a diver, they disapproved it, and from there we just didn't get along well after that. The same thing happened aboard the USS Tripoli.[*] I wanted to be a diver.

Q: What motivated you to want to be a diver?

Master Chief Brashear: Well, what first motivated me to be a diver happened at Key West, Florida. We parted the lower block on a buoy, and they brought out the YSD, which is a yard diving craft.[†] The guy put on a face mask and a shallow-water diving rig and fixed our block. That was my first encounter with seeing a guy dive.

Then when I requested it on the USS Palau, it was disapproved, and they transferred me to the USS Tripoli. Well, when the USS Tripoli was anchored off the coast of Corpus

---

[*] The USS Tripoli (CVE-64) was commissioned 31 October 1943. She had a displacement of 7,800 tons, was 512 feet long, 65 feet in the beam, an extreme width of 108 feet on the flight deck, and had a draft of 22 feet. She had a top speed of 19 knots and could accommodate approximately 27 aircraft.

[†] YSD--self-propelled seaplane wrecking derrick.

Christi, Texas, one of our aircraft, an old TBM, rolled off of the jettison ramp.* This time they brought out a barge and made it into a moor and dressed a guy up in a deep-sea diving suit. This was where I said, "Now, this is the best thing since sliced bread. I've got to be a deep-sea diver." So I started requesting, requesting, requesting to be a deep-sea diver. I finally got into school in 1954.

Q: What do you remember about the operations of these ships while you were on board? Where did you go?

Master Chief Brashear: While I was on board the USS Palau, we never deployed to the Med or anyplace like that. We would go to Key West, New York, Mayport, places like that. Nine months later, I was gone off of that ship and went to the USS Tripoli. While on board the USS Tripoli, we deployed to northern Europe, the Med, the Pacific. We did a lot of steaming.

Q: You were getting some of what the recruiters promised: to join the Navy and see the world.

Master Chief Brashear: Yes, and I saw a lot of the world on board the USS Tripoli.

Q: What are some of the highlights you remember from those ports?

Master Chief Brashear: Well, the port I remember best was Copenhagen, Denmark. I think I enjoyed that most of any port.

Q: What about Copenhagen appealed to you?

---

* The TBM Avenger was a carrier-based torpedo bomber that first joined the fleet during World War II.

Master Chief Brashear: The people. The people were very nice there. They would invite you in for milk and Danish, pastry, most of all. And they treated you nice. If you met a young lady, she would invite you over to the house. I was on the boxing team during those days, and I was jogging in the neighborhood. One day I met a young lady who was a wrestler, and we started dating. When the ship would go into Bremerhaven, Germany, I'd catch a train and go up to Copenhagen, Denmark, to see this young lady. I thought Copenhagen was the best port I ever got into.

Q: Understandably. Tell me more about the boxing team, please.

Master Chief Brashear: Well, I was on the boxing team for about three years on board the Tripoli. I beat everybody on the Tripoli when they held the smokers. Then my first encounter off of the ship was in Sheepshead Bay, New York.[*] That's where I met Sugar Ray Robinson, and he was going to teach us how to fight.[†] And I fought a Marine there at Sheepshead Bay. He was a good influence on us.

Q: What did you learn from him?

Master Chief Brashear: Well, I learned from Sugar Ray how to throw jabs, not drop your right hand, like he said I was doing a lot of times, just a good defensive type of fighting. But it was a lot different fighting amateur and fighting pro. In the amateur fights, you've got to fight three minutes of every round. You can't study your opponent to see where he's coming from, to use those words. You've got to get out there and fight. But I learned a lot from Sugar Ray, keeping your hands up, jabbing.

Q: Well, that also would appeal to your sense of adventure.

---

[*] Sheepshead Bay is an indentation in the southwest shore of Long Island. It is in the southern section of Brooklyn, one of the boroughs of New York City.
[†] Walker Smith was a stylish black boxer who fought under the name Sugar Ray Robinson in the 1940s and 1950s. At different times he was the world welterweight champion and middleweight champion.

Master Chief Brashear: Yes.

Q: Did the team, as a whole, do well?

Master Chief Brashear: Yes, we did quite well. I recall people like Luzon, who was the heavyweight champion of the Navy. And Don Lee was the heavyweight champion of the Navy. I fought for the light-heavyweight championship of the East Coast and lost. But the team, as a whole, did quite well.

Q: Did being on the boxing team help your feeling toward the ship, or were you still unhappy? Did that give you more loyalty to the Tripoli?

Master Chief Brashear: Yes, I guess in some aspects it did, because they were very interested in sports in those days, and they looked out quite a bit for the fighters and athletes.

Q: At what point did you feel that you needed more education?

Master Chief Brashear: Well, I realized I needed more education right after I made third class boatswain's mate. That's when I enrolled in the USAFI courses, I guess, they had in those days.*

Q: Correspondence courses.

Master Chief Brashear: Correspondence courses. So I studied quite a bit in that.

Q: Were there any instructors on board, or did you have to do it all yourself?

---

* USAFI--United States Armed Forces Institute.

Master Chief Brashear: All yourself. It wasn't like it is in today's Navy.

Q: That's a tough way to go to high school.

Master Chief Brashear: Right. And I took my GED test and passed it in 1960.[*] My first phase of diving school didn't require a high school diploma. But when I got into mixed-gas diving, that's when they required a high school diploma.

Q: That's a good motivation to get you to do something.

Master Chief Brashear: Yes.

Q: When did you make second class?

Master Chief Brashear: I made second class boatswain's mate in 1953.

Q: So just before you went to diving school.

Master Chief Brashear: Right before I went to diving school.

Q: So were you essentially just at Key West in the squadron and then those two ships before you went to the school?

Master Chief Brashear: Yes.

Q: Anything else to remember about those experiences before you talk about the diving school?

---

[*] GED--general educational development, a test that is essentially equivalent to the knowledge expected of a high school graduate.

Master Chief Brashear: Well, it was an exciting experience in different areas, but I think once I started pursuing to be a diver, I think that's where my heart and my goals were. But I was aboard the Tripoli from 1951 to '54, and it was a good ship.

Q: What kinds of planes was she operating basically?

Master Chief Brashear: She was a ferry type, MSTS.[*]

Q: I see.

Chief Brashear: We would ferry just any kind of planes that somebody had to ferry. We'd load up in New Jersey and go to Bremerhaven, Germany, or Copenhagen, Denmark, or somewhere in France and places like that. Then we deployed to the West Coast, and we were doing the same thing over there.

Q: Did you get out to the Korean War zone?

Master Chief Brashear: Yes, we did.

Q: What do you recall about that?

Master Chief Brashear: Well, we were just off of the coast of Korea, and there wasn't too much to see.

Q: Again, just transporting airplanes?

---

[*] The Tripoli had been out of commission from 1946 to 1952. When she was recommissioned on 5 January 1952, she was assigned to the Military Sea Transportation Service.

Master Chief Brashear: Just transporting airplanes.

Q: Well, I'm sure that really developed you as a boatswain's mate, all that time on board ship.

Master Chief Brashear: Yes, we did a lot of things. That's when they had the old paravane gear for minesweeping. I was getting to be a well-rounded second class boatswain's mate when I got off of that ship. Plus, when we'd be in port, I'd go to LSTs to get my practical factors marked off, to see how they operated the bow doors, to see how they did a lot of other things.* I was determined to go places.

Q: Well, and one mark of a well-rounded second class boatswain's mate is that he knows how to hold his coffee cup while others are getting the job done.

Master Chief Brashear: Yes. [Laughter]

Q: Leadership and supervision.

Master Chief Brashear: Yes, that's right. I was a young boatswain's mate, and I had a division on board the Tripoli. I was the second division petty officer, and I was 20-some years old. I had a couple of third class boatswain's mates in the division that had 17-18 years in the Navy.

Q: That's a long way from being a sharecropper in Kentucky.

Master Chief Brashear: Yes, it was--a long ways.

Q: What do you recall about the diving school?

---

* LST--tank landing ship, an amphibious warfare ship capable of putting her bow directly onto a beach, opening bow doors, and lowering a bow ramp to permit vehicles to exit.

Master Chief Brashear: The diving school was in Bayonne, New Jersey. That involved a lot of psychological stress, a lot of hard work getting through that diving school. When I reported in to the diving school, the training officer thought I was reporting there as a steward or a cook. When he found out that I was there to be a student, he called me in, and he said, "Well, I don't know how the rest of the students are going to accept you. As a matter of fact, I don't even think you will make it through the school. We haven't had a colored guy come through here before."

Q: That's a real welcome, isn't it?

Master Chief Brashear: Yes. And he said, "Well, but that's what you're here for."

I said, "Certainly that's what I'm here for."

Then I had about a week to hang around before the school started. One of the chief boatswain's mates needed some wire spliced. So I spliced a lot of wire and did a lot of work before the school started. When school started, somebody in the school was trying to get next to me. They would put notes on my bunk: "We're going to drown you today, nigger!" "We don't want any nigger divers." So one day, I was going to quit, but I heard from a man named Rutherford; he was a first class boatswain's mate from Arkansas.

Q: Was he on the staff of the school?

Master Chief Brashear: Yes. He was on the staff. He said, "Meet me at the dungaree bar this afternoon, Brashear." That's when you could go drink beer in dungarees. So I met him at the dungaree bar, and he said, "I hear you're going to quit."

I said, "Yeah, well, I'm not going to take this mess."

It made him mad, see. And he said, "You son-of-a-bitch. I can't whip you, but I'll fight you every day if you quit." He said, "Those notes are not hurting you. No one is doing a thing to you. Show them you're a better man than they are."

And then we started drinking beer, see. And before you know it, man, I perked up. [Laughter]

Q: It sounds as if people came into your life when you needed them.

Master Chief Brashear: Yes. So I perked up, and I continued on in school. I graduated number 16 out of a class of 17. I wasn't the anchor man. I was the first black man to graduate from that school. [Laughter]

Q: What do you remember about the actual training? What sorts of things did you study?

Master Chief Brashear: Well, in diving school in those days, you started off with your regular PT in the morning.* Then the first week was orientation. The second week was physics. And then diving medicine and diving physics, of course. Then you had a period there of nothing but just pure diving. They call it pure diving, where you do all your projects: your flanges, your underwater welding, your underwater cutting and just basic underwater tools, hydraulics, and what have you. That was for four weeks. Then you had two weeks of demolition. We studied how to make boom-booms using primer cord, TNT. During those days it was composition C3, a plastic explosive.

So we had the demolition, and then the last few weeks we had salvage. That's when you learned all about beach gear: the mechanical purchases to pull stranded vessels off the beach, belly lift gear, to lift heavy objects off of the bottom and, again, putting in splices-- metallic splices and all that. That was salvage.

Q: Did your eighth-grade education handicap you during the classroom work?

Master Chief Brashear: No, it did not. Believe it or not, I adapted. I picked up that training. I made good marks in the classroom. I'd write good papers.

---

* PT--physical training.

Q: Because you were really motivated to do this.

Master Chief Brashear: Right. I never flunked an exam in salvage school.

Q: Great.

Master Chief Brashear: Not even physics. And you couldn't use a slipstick or a calculator either.* [Laughter] But I never flunked an exam. Some of the guys flunked and did a makeup. Well, I didn't do a lot of other things in diving school, either. I didn't go over on the beach and steam at night. I studied, because I knew they were looking at me. I couldn't fail, because I think if I had failed one exam, I think they would have put me out of school with the attitude there. I didn't fail a thing. And I was on the diving station the whole time.

    The diving school is geared to put a lot of stress on you. I know that, because I've been an instructor in diving school myself. It's geared to see how it can break you down, see how it can get you angry. One time I was putting a breastplate on one of the divers and dropped a wing nut. The chief saw it. So he made me walk around the parking lot with a deep-sea diving helmet on my head. [Laughter] Just walk around the parking lot for dropping that nut, and then I had to come back and do push-ups with that deep-sea diving helmet on me.

Q: I bet you were in good physical condition.

Master Chief Brashear: Oh, yes. I was in fantastic condition.

Q: Well, staying in shape has been an interest of yours your whole life, hasn't it?

---

* "Slipstick" was a slang term of a slide rule, a device later essentially replaced by hand-held calculators.

Master Chief Brashear: Yes. Even today, I'm in good shape. I go to the gym, work out, and fight a couple of rounds. I've always been a nut for physical fitness.

Q: Well, please describe that experience of going down in the heavy suit.

Master Chief Brashear: Well, every dive is different, and when you get down there in the suit, you can't see. The lights would go out in Bayonne, New Jersey, after you put your head below the surface. It's just a different situation. You get a different feeling down there. It's a different world. Then you're down there, and you know how the people are thinking about you up topside. You know they've got to pull you up. But you've got to have faith in those people up there too. Even though they don't like you or they want to see you washed out, they're not going to do anything to you down there. So you've got to depend on those folks to bring you up.

Q: Did you ever have any feelings of doubt about that?

Master Chief Brashear: I never had any feelings of doubt that they would do something to me down there--never. My faith didn't think a man would be that calm under that load. Plus it wouldn't only be him. Someone in the chain of command would have to investigate. So I never had that fear.

Q: Well, that was certainly a help.

Master Chief Brashear: No, I never, never had that fear. I always felt that they would be tending and taking care of me as a diver like they would somebody else.

Q: Did you have any feelings of discomfort? Certainly being strapped into that heavy gear and breathing through a hose is different from being on land.

Master Chief Brashear: No, I just felt comfortable in it. No claustrophobia. No excitement. No anxiety. Nothing like buttoning up in that deep-sea diving suit.

Q: Maybe this was because this was what you'd been asking for for so many years, and you finally got it.

Master Chief Brashear: And I just psyched myself up and was so overwhelmed to be a diver, it just didn't build up in me. But the psychologists say claustrophobia is there in every person. Just like diving four atmospheres, you're going to get a little bit of nitrogen narcosis. They say claustrophobia is there, but I did not experience it.

Q: How far down did you go during that training course?

Master Chief Brashear: The deepest place up there in Bayonne was 64-65 feet when we were making our dives. They would try to extend your bottom time so that you were required to make a couple of decompression stops. It was mostly ten-foot stops.

Q: This was to avoid the bends.

Master Chief Brashear: Yes. Having the bends means nitrogen bubbles in the bloodstream or the tissues.

Q: And so it's a matter of coming up gradually to avoid that.

Master Chief Brashear: Yes, to put off the bubbles in the form of a gas instead of it coming out the solution in the form of a bubble. That's the purpose of the staged decompression.

Q: Did you ever have any problems in your career with the bends?

Master Chief Brashear: No. I was treated one time for the bends in Hawaii. I got off the Tripoli's boxing team when I was a youngster, and then I got back on the boxing team as a chief petty officer in Hawaii. My shoulders were swollen after a deep dive out there on the West Coast. And we thought it was the bends, and I was treated. But my shoulders were swollen when I come up, too, and I was still hurting. So I guess I just got hit so hard in the boxing ring, but they treated it as a doubtful case.

Q: Well, probably better to be safe than sorry.

Master Chief Brashear: Oh, sure. I treat all doubtful cases myself. But they treated me and soaked me the required time, and when I came up, I was still hurting just like I did before I went down in the hyperbaric-recompression chamber.

Q: Are there any of the specific techniques that you remember from Bayonne that we should put on the record. For example, what do you remember about welding and demolition?

Master Chief Brashear: I remember what the instructor said about my underwater welding grades in Bayonne, New Jersey. He said they were the best welds they ever saw anybody do underwater.

Q: What makes a good weld underwater?

Master Chief Brashear: Judging how to advance your rod--that makes a good weld, and how steady you are with your rod, because it's a self-consuming method. You have to touch the metal, and you're welding right inside of a little bubble. That's what makes a good weld. It's just a technique you can develop how you advance your rod, whether it's going up, vertical, overhead, or what have you.

Q: Well, welding is something that takes some skill in any event. It seems to me it would be that much harder underwater.

Master Chief Brashear: Yes. It's amazing that once you did the underwater welding, seems like in all the diving schools, that people that are not hull technicians or shipfitters make better marks in underwater welding than the hull technicians and the shipfitters.

Q: Why do you think that is?

Master Chief Brashear: Well, I think it's like, for instance, the shipfitters and the damage controlmen make better marks in seamanship sometimes than the boatswain's mates because they don't listen. They think, "Well, I'm a welder up here on the surface. I know what I'm doing." So they have a tendency not to be retrained. Like for me, I didn't listen either when I was in a seamanship class in diving school. I would read something into a question that was not even there, see. You're just overconfident. So I think that's what happens to the shipfitters. They don't listen, and they just don't want to be retaught how to weld.

Q: What do you have for a light source when you're working down below?

Master Chief Brashear: In muddy black water, you don't have any light source. A light only works in clear water. You just feel. If you want to weld something and you can't see it, you feel it, and then you weld it. That's where good mechanical ability comes in, you see. You've got to be mechanically inclined. If you're not, you're not going to get your job done. That's very important in being a deep-sea diver.

Q: What do you remember about the explosives work?

Master Chief Brashear: Well, I remember in the explosive work, we knocked some windows out of some people's houses in Swinburne Island.* [Laughter]

So we got smart and learned a lot. And the instructors would have us put two or three pounds of explosives together and go over and shoot it. Well, you know, we were good. We had learned a lot, and so we put in a little more explosive. Well, this one particular day, the clouds were a little low, so we mixed up some C3 and some dynamite and went over the hill and shot it. The sound wave went up and hit those clouds and blew against the hill and knocked out the people's windows, see. [Laughter] And the diving school got a telephone call.

Q: I'll bet it did.

Master Chief Brashear: So that's what I learned. That was exciting about that job.

Q: Sounds like you were getting a little cocky at that point.

Master Chief Brashear: Oh, yes. You always get a little cocky; you learn a little too much and get dangerous. When you do a demolition job on a cloudy day you have to cut your explosives down if you've got a residential area or buildings somewhere, because, see, it will only go up so far.

Q: Was safety a big part of the curriculum?

Master Chief Brashear: You know, they didn't stress safety like we do now. We weren't that safe. And, believe it or not, we didn't have that many accidents. A lot of times, we didn't change the oil in our compressors or the filters or the loofa sponges like we were supposed to and get our air analyzed like we do today. We just didn't pay that much

---

* Swinburne Island is between Brooklyn and Staten Island; it is about three miles south of the Verrazano Narrows Bridge.

attention to it. We would breathe air off a compressor, and we'd come up and we'd feel oil on our lips. We weren't as safety-conscious as we are now in the diving community.

Q: Was it straight air you were getting, or a higher proportion of oxygen?

Master Chief Brashear: No, salvage school was just straight air. I'll tell you the story about breathing oxygen. But we were breathing straight air, and if our loofa sponges weren't cleaning up well enough, we would put Kotex, rags, anything in our oil separators to try to take out some of the oil.

Q: After you had been there a while and proved yourself, were you accepted better?

Master Chief Brashear: I started being accepted very well about the last two weeks of the school. And the night of the graduation, I was accepted very well.

Q: How long was the course?

Master Chief Brashear: Sixteen weeks. Yes, I was accepted very well.

Q: After you and Rutherford went out for the beers, did he help you along with the training, give you some advice and encouragement and that sort of thing?

Master Chief Brashear: No, he did not.

Q: It was just that one encounter?

Master Chief Brashear: Just that one encounter. I was like everybody else the next morning. When I graduated from school, I went for years without seeing Rutherford.

Eventually I ran into him in Hawaii. He was the XO of one of the ARS-type ships.* I forget which one it was, maybe the Bolster. We met up over there and swapped sea stories. This was in Hawaii in 1961.

Q: Anything more to mention about the diving school?

Master Chief Brashear: Well, no. I think I've just about covered it. It was a stressful, psychological job to get through the school.

Q: I'm sure that was a great feeling of satisfaction for you.

Master Chief Brashear: Well, when I graduated from that school, I could have stepped over the building. That was one good feeling when they called me up there and handed me that diploma. And it was sort of exciting, too, the way they did it. I was graduated number 16 out of a class of 17. And, of course, they gave the anchor man a spiel about the fact that he could have held the class back. Shoots was his name. Shoots and I were standing there looking at each other, didn't know which one was going to be the anchor man, because they already told me about the anchor man before graduation. So they paused and left us, and we were looking around at each other. [Laughter]

Q: They built a little suspense.

Master Chief Brashear: Yes. So I was number 16 out of a class of 17, but we had started with 32 people.

Q: So you were really 16 out of 32.

---

* Lieutenant Harry M. Rutherford, USN, a limited duty officer.

Master Chief Brashear: Yes. But you have to finish the school, so I was 16 out of 17 out of the graduating. We lost almost half of that class.

Q: What were the living conditions like when you were there?

Master Chief Brashear: Terrible.

Q: Were you in barracks?

Master Chief Brashear: Barracks with broken-out windows, and the window panes weren't making tack. One time it snowed, and we had to stuff blankets in the windows to keep the snow out. The living conditions were terrible.

Q: Was this there at the supply center in Bayonne?

Master Chief Brashear: No, we didn't live at the supply center. We lived in the old building right on the pier head where we dove. They said, "If you're going to be divers, you must be rugged."

Q: Well, Bayonne is not a garden spot, anyway. [Laughter]

Master Chief Brashear: That's right. That's right.

Q: Did you have any choice in where you would go for your first duty assignment as a diver?

Master Chief Brashear: No, I didn't have any choice. I was only there TAD from the Tripoli, so I returned to her.* Let me tell you what happened to me, though, before I returned to the USS Tripoli. Now, this is how I was accepted.

The Bennington had lost 16,000 rounds of ammunition. This was after graduation, but Rutherford recommended that I stay and get my orders extended to make up the diving crew that they were going out there to pick up the 16,000 rounds of ammunition. So I stayed there about three months after my graduation diving on this ammunition.

Q: Where was the ammunition?

Master Chief Brashear: It was right off of Gravesend Bay, New York.† It was just a few miles from NAD Earle.‡

Q: What were the circumstances of losing the ammunition? Do you remember?

Master Chief Brashear: Well, the Bennington was going into the yard, so she went out there to anchor to off-load ammunition.§ While she was there, a first class boatswain's mate had a barge load of ammunition. He said that he saw his old tug listing. The barge broke in half, and 16,000 rounds of ammunition went down on the bottom. I picked up and accounted for all but a few rounds. I was on the complete job.

Q: What size ammunition was it?

Master Chief Brashear: 3-inch/50.

---

* TAD--temporary additional duty.
† Gravesend Bay is an indentation in southwest Brooklyn, between the Verrazano Narrows Bridge and Coney island.
‡ Naval Ammunition Depot, Earle, New Jersey.
§ The USS Bennington (CVS-20) was in the New York Naval Shipyard from June 1954 to March 1955 for a major conversion, including angled flight deck and hurricane bow.

Q: That's a lot of bullets.

Master Chief Brashear: That's a lot of bullets. What we did was rig up a barge and put it in a four-point moor. And we made a big, huge basket, and we lowered that basket to the bottom. It was in 72 feet of water. Then we'd go down there in a deep-sea rig and prowl through the mud, just loading that basket with 3-inch/50 ammunition. We'd work until we couldn't work anymore, and then we'd come up and go down again. We accounted for practically all of it.

Q: Could you see it at all?

Master Chief Brashear: Couldn't see a thing. Visibility was zero.

Q: How heavy did one of those projectiles feel under that much water?

Master Chief Brashear: Well, wobbling through the mud, it felt heavy, and it was muddy. It was muddy--mud over your knees.

Q: So you had a crane then that picked up the basket?

Master Chief Brashear: Picked up the basket and transferred it to another barge and unloaded it and put the basket down there again.

Q: How long did all that take?

Master Chief Brashear: We were out there about three months, three and a half months. You know, we'd have to shift our barge back and forth. Then sometimes the current would be so swift that you couldn't dive but certain periods of the day, even putting on two weight belts. That was another thing; we'd just disregard the safety rules.

Q: Why?

Master Chief Brashear: To get the job done. We tried to get down through that current and hang on, just hanging on and picking up ammunition and hanging on to our descent line or hanging on to that basket. Sometimes the current would be so strong that we'd wear two weight belts.

Q: Do you remember when you worked on that ammunition?

Master Chief Brashear: October, November, and December of 1954. I left to go back to the ship about the 18th day of December.

Q: Did you have a chance for New York liberty during that period?

Master Chief Brashear: I lived with my first wife on 126th Street in New York.

Q: That was convenient.

Master Chief Brashear: Yes.

Q: Well, please tell me about her. How had you met her?

Master Chief Brashear: I met her back in Elizabethtown, Kentucky, when she was going to high school. All the family knew her; she used to hang around with my sisters when she was a little girl and we'd go to Elizabethtown. We started dating and got married in '52. Then she finished beauty school and was a cosmetologist. We went to New York in 1953 and lived on 126th Street, because the USS Tripoli was homeported out of New York. When I got my orders to go to diving school, the ship was in Mobile, Alabama, and I came back over and started my diving school.

Q: What was your wife's name?

Master Chief Brashear: Her name was Junetta, and we stayed married for quite some time.

Q: Did you have regrets about going back to the ship after this exciting work on the ammunition?

Master Chief Brashear: Yes. I didn't want to go back to the USS Tripoli, because there were no divers aboard.

Q: What was the point of sending you back then?

Master Chief Brashear: Because I was TAD. So I went back there in December of '54, and the exec, I guess, pulled some strings for me. I left in March of '55 to a diving ship, an ARS, the USS Opportune.*

Q: Now you were really getting into something you wanted.

Master Chief Brashear: Yes, so I reported aboard the USS Opportune early in 1955.

Q: Where was she?

Master Chief Brashear: She was homeported in San Juan, Puerto Rico. But she'd already got orders to change home ports to Norfolk, Virginia. I went aboard the USS Opportune and did a lot of diving jobs while I was aboard.

---

* The salvage ship USS Opportune (ARS-41) was commissioned on 5 October 1945. Characteristics included displacement, 1,990 tons; length, 214 feet; beam, 43 feet; draft, 14 feet; top speed, 16 knots; armament, two twin 40-millimeter guns.

Q: Well, please tell me some of the ones you remember.

Master Chief Brashear: A gas barge sank in 86 feet of water off of Charleston, South Carolina, and we went down there to raise her. That was our first salvage job.

Q: How did you go about that?

Master Chief Brashear: Well, we went about that by patching and blowing, using the blowing method. We'd blow a hole in it for it to level out on the bottom. It was a YN or YON, and on the decks you had three hatches each side, port and starboard. So we patched it, and then we'd take off each one of those hatches and put a blow and a vent pipe on it. When we made her tight, then we pumped air into it using Leroy compressors.

But when you're blowing something like that, you've got to be very careful. The first time we raised it, we didn't watch our gauges well enough and got too much pressure in it and ruptured her seams, and she went back down. What you're supposed to do and when you start blowing is start cutting down on your air so you won't have too much air pressure inside.

Q: Just bring it up gradually.

Master Chief Brashear: Bring it up gradually. But we brought it up a little too fast, and she ruptured and went back down. Then we step-raised it and patched it and pumped it after that.

Q: How many men were involved in the job?

Master Chief Brashear: Well, an ARS has about 18 divers aboard, total, and the crew of ARS is about 100-105.

Q: Sounds like a diver's heaven.

Master Chief Brashear: That's a diver's paradise; I remember that. I was a salvage diver, and, of course, you had first-class divers and second-class divers. We didn't have a master in those days on board the Opportune. I think the Navy had only about six or seven masters during those days. So that was my first salvage job on board the Opportune. And there's quite a bit involved when you're salvaging something. Even salvaging a wreck, it's always miserable, it's always dangerous, and the weather seems like it's always bad. There's no pleasant salvage job.

Then we were on a training mission off the coast here out in the Virginia Capes laying beach gear. Remember an aircraft called the S-2?[*]

Q: Antisubmarine plane.

Master Chief Brashear: Yes. We were in a two-point moor, getting ready to do some seamanship evolution, and we heard the plane sputter and mutter. Finally, she crashed. Well, Stillwell, we put ourselves in a dangerous situation. We took a work boat and put bottles of oxygen in it, because it was too shallow to get the ship in. We put bottles of oxygen and a gauge on an oxygen bottle and dove and salvaged those people in that airplane on pure oxygen. And there was grease all over the water. Can you imagine diving?

Q: How deep was it?

Master Chief Brashear: Fifteen, sixteen feet. You could see part of the plane sticking out. But we were diving on pure oxygen around all of that oil and grease.

Q: Why pure oxygen?

---

[*] In 1962 the Grumman S2F Tracker was redesignated S-2.

Master Chief Brashear: We didn't want to put a big old compressor in our little work boat. We thought we were doing the right thing and dove on pure oxygen. You know, oxygen could have blown, and we could have blown up. We worked over there for a couple of weeks and brought a YSD over there and picked that plane up, put it on the ship, and got the bodies out.

Q: What did you have to do in those two weeks to get the thing ready for lifting?

Master Chief Brashear: We had to put wire straps onto different structures and pick up the plane, piece by piece. When we would pick some of it up, well, it would break apart and go back down. Sometimes you'd have to go down and take a choker strap and put it around part of the plane and pick it up, piece by piece by piece. Then whoever the safety officer is on those jobs always wants the black box. You don't care about the rest of the plane but that black box. Then you'd have to get out there in the mud and search for that black box.

Q: By feel again.

Master Chief Brashear: By feel. And it's very, very dangerous diving in those situations, because you'll cut yourself in cool water, and you won't know you are cut. You'll cut your hands, and it's very hazardous.

Q: Did you wear gloves?

Master Chief Brashear: You wore gloves, but you still could cut your hands once you get so cold, you know. So you cut your suit and were getting wet, but you couldn't feel it.

Q: What time of the year was that?

Master Chief Brashear: I forget just what month it was, but it was dead wintertime.

Q: What were some of the other jobs you had?

Master Chief Brashear: We had a salvage job up in Argentia, Newfoundland. We pulled a ship off the beach up there, had about six sets of beach gear on this one ship. I don't know if you ever heard of him or not, but the best salvage master we ever had in the Navy was named Thurman; people called him Bulldog Thurman.* He was a full commander and had a great big old face. We called him Bulldog Thurman because he looked like his dog.

We had about six sets of beach gear laid on this old ship, and my set of beach gear was blue. You know, you have to color-code your beach gear blue, yellow, and red, because you get so much of it laid. So I was heaving around on all my beach gear with two D-8 cats way up the beach.†

So I kept telling Thurman, "Blue got a heavy, heavy strain."

He said, "Heave around."

I kept saying, "Blue's got a heavy strain."

This was about 3:00 in the morning. My beach gear was that high off of the pier.

Q: Two or three feet.

Master Chief Brashear: Yes, but he kept telling me to heave around. Finally, it carried away and looked like a fire on the pier, all 2,400 feet of wire on each purchase was just going around those sheaves. I jumped off on the pier, and old Thurman threw a shackle at me. [Laughter]

Q: You warned him.

---

* Commander Robert K. Thurman, USN.
† Cats--Catarpiller tractors.

Master Chief Brashear: He threw a shackle at me and said, "You dumb son-of-a-bitch" But that was a good job. We were trying to winch her, and I never will forget Thurman for that.

Q: What kind of a ship was it?

Master Chief Brashear: It was an old merchant ship on a C-2 hull, that had run aground up there off of Newfoundland.[*]

Q: That was a pretty good-sized vessel.

Master Chief Brashear: Yes, it was a good-sized vessel.

Q: So you didn't really need diving so much for that, did you?

Master Chief Brashear: Yes, you always need divers when you salvage something. You have to survey the bottom and plant your buoys. Then you have to swim a channel out to find which way you want to take the ship once she becomes lively and know the direction you're going to pull. You, survey the hull, make sure there's no rupture, and then you've got to get inside of it. So you always have to have your divers.

Q: What sort of vessel did you have doing the tugging on these shackles or on these lines?

Master Chief Brashear: We had the ARS out pulling out in that direction when she became lively. But to winch it, see, you fairlead it to the beach and use Caterpillars to twist or break that friction.[†] Do you know what I mean?

---

[*] A typical C-2 cargo ship was about 450 feet long and about 6,000-7,000 gross tons.
[†] Fairlead is a fitting, such as a block or pulley, that provides a friction-free passage for a line or cable. Fairlead is also a term to describe an unhampered route for a line or cable.

Q: Yes.

Master Chief Brashear: But the ARS was out off of the stern of the ship when she became lively and came off the beach. Then she could take control of it. That's when you trip out. So, see, you had to have your channel how you wanted it to go.

Q: Well, you probably had to check the underwater hull, too, to make sure she was seaworthy before you pulled her off.

Master Chief Brashear: Yes. All that you could get to. And when she came off the beach, then you'd have to inspect the hull again to make sure she didn't rupture herself.

Q: How long did that project take?

Master Chief Brashear: We were there about three weeks. But the biggest part was getting rigged and waiting for the right tide. You had to get your equipment in there and get it over on the beach. You use some heavy equipment when you start rigging for salvage.

Q: What other jobs do you recall?

Master Chief Brashear: Well, let's go back to the Opportune. We had a job at Labrador, where we had cold, cold weather. We had to lay an underwater fuel line into the Air Force base there in Saglek Bay, Labrador. So we got the fuel line laid, no problem. Then the ship was coming up to make an anchor and tie up to the buoy. He was going to drop his anchor out here and then drift over to the buoy and then make up to the buoy to hook up his fuel line. But he lost his anchor, so we had to go find that anchor for that old merchant ship. The diver was a first-class petty officer name of Luzon, and we were exceeding the capabilities for a diver in the shallow-water suit.

Q: What do you mean exceeding the capabilities?

Master Chief Brashear: At that time, we weren't supposed to dive but 60 feet in a face mask. We were down about almost 100. Well, when you get down to that depth, you don't have the volume in the hose to get the air down to you. Do you know what I mean?

Q: That's something to be concerned about.

Master Chief Brashear: Yes. So he dove at almost 100 feet in that shallow-water gear, that old "can-do" spirit. And we gave Luzon a signal by tugging on the air hose and lifeline, and he answered. Then we gave Luzon a signal, and he didn't answer. We gave him another signal; he didn't answer. So we brought Luzon up; I was the tender. There he was--passed out, no mask on. He was starting to turn blue, so we gave him artificial respiration and brought him around.

Q: That makes your point, again, about the safety being sort of lax back then.

Master Chief Brashear: Yes, it was. Yes.

Q: Well, please tell me more about the teamwork that's involved in a dive.

Master Chief Brashear: Diving requires tremendous teamwork. You've got to have teamwork, and you've got to know each other's capabilities. You've got to know a lot about your fellow man. It just requires a lot of teamwork to make a job run.

Q: What are some of the positions that are involved? You talked about the man tending the line up top. What else?

Master Chief Brashear: Well, each diver requires two tenders. The minimum you can have for diving is four. You need the tenders, a timekeeper, and a supervisor. That's what makes up a diving team, the minimum. But in your deep-sea diving mode, then you require more personnel. You have to have a compressor watch. You have to have two tenders. You've got to have a supervisor. Plus, your ship has got to be in a two-point moor. It just requires quite a few people.

Q: How reliable was the equipment back then?

Master Chief Brashear: The equipment was very reliable. As a matter of fact, in the 1970s I was the master diver at the Naval Safety Center for two years, and we researched records. We went back as far as we could go in diving and found only two equipment failures that caused accidents. Most of it was personnel errors.

Q: What are some of the kinds of personnel errors that you encounter?

Master Chief Brashear: Not following safety precautions. Most of the time they don't follow the decompression profile, or they'll dive a person that is tired, or they'll dive a man that is just not physically fit to be diving that one particular day, or weather conditions. A lot of things are built into a safety precaution in a dive.

Q: Sounds like that "can-do" spirit can get in the way of safety.

Master Chief Brashear: That "can-do" spirit can do you in, and I'm a good example of that with my leg. Sometimes you have an accident if the master diver doesn't analyze his gas properly, or he doesn't have his air analyzed like he's supposed to. It's things of this nature. When I was at the safety center, I investigated about 80 accidents a year--and it was all personnel error.

Q: Does a lot of that have to do with insufficient training?

Master Chief Brashear: No. They get the proper training. They get very good training. It's just oversight, overlooking things.

Q: Carelessness?

Master Chief Brashear: Carelessness and taking shortcuts to get the job done.

Q: So you've got to strike a proper balance between getting that job done and getting a job done safely.

Master Chief Brashear: Yes, you have, very much so.

Q: What was the relationship between the divers and the ship's company personnel on board the Opportune?

Master Chief Brashear: There would be a little friction between them at times, because in those days, on a hazardous dive--you could make any dive hazardous--they drew $5.50 an hour. Well, the divers would be out there working around the clock. That was tying up the ship's company guy, who was getting just his regular pay. There would be a little friction, you know, that the divers are drawing all this fabulous pay and, "I'm out here, you know. I'm staying up, I'm on the job, but I'm not getting that pay."

Q: And maybe he's being held up from liberty.

Master Chief Brashear: He could be held up from liberty, or some diving job would come up just right at liberty call on weekends, and the ship had to get under way. So sometimes it would build up a little friction. But, there again, the diving school is open for everybody.

Q: Yes, indeed.

Master Chief Brashear: It's there for everybody.

Q: Were the officers in the ship experienced salvage people?

Master Chief Brashear: Yes. The ARSs require four experienced salvage officers, and if they're not experienced, they will get it once they get aboard there and start working.

Q: Would the skipper, for example, be a mustang?*

Master Chief Brashear: In those days, they all were mustangs, but now they have changed the rules. A lot of the ARS skippers are not mustangs. But, gee, I served with mustangs up until the '70s. Every one of them was an ex-chief boatswain's mate, ex-chief signalman, some type of mustang.

Q: Really knew the job.

Master Chief Brashear: Yes, they did. Yes, they did. Could get the job done. Although I was with a youngster, too, very young--he's a four-striper now--Charlie Bonham.† He was a great young officer. He was our skipper, just fantastic. And Zarr was nice.‡ I've seen a lot of those guys come out and didn't know what an ARS was, but they made some good skippers. Then the old saying got around, "Maybe we should have had managers on those ships before we had those technicians." [Laughter] He depended on us a lot, but he was a fantastic man. He didn't know anything about salvage, but he was a good commanding officer.

---

* "Mustang" is Navy slang for a former enlisted man who has risen through the ranks to become an officer.
† Lieutenant Commander Charlie L. Bonham, USN, later commanded the USS Recovery (ARS-43), 1972-74.
‡ Don Wayne Zarr, a former electrician's mate, retired in 1970 as a chief warrant officer-4.

Q: What other jobs do you remember from the Opportune?

Master Chief Brashear: Well, that was about it. We had small jobs like changing propellers and doing screw jobs and inspections and regular old salvage work.

Q: How did you spend your time in between the salvage jobs?

Master Chief Brashear: We would tow targets a lot, and that's what we would do mostly. And then we would go out and have gunnery training and have to have our regular drills.

Q: But you were mostly just a passenger for that.

Master Chief Brashear: No, not a passenger. I was in a repair party, did other training required, plus doing paper work.

Q: I see. Well, did you then do boatswain's mate-type work when the ship would be on that kind of a mission?

Master Chief Brashear: Oh, yes. See, diving is not a rate; it's a specialty. I was a regular boatswain's mate when we weren't diving. There again, when the crew would be talking about divers getting pay that they weren't, hey, I'd have to get out and work as a deck boatswain's mate. Then if a diving job came up, I'd have to go do that too, see. So I was a regular boatswain's mate.

Q: Well, along with some of this resentment they had about your extra pay, they probably had to respect your abilities.

Master Chief Brashear: Yes. Yes, they did.

Q: Did you make first class on board that ship?

Master Chief Brashear: Yes, I made first class on board in 1955 in Argentia, Newfoundland. My wife and I didn't have any kids in those days, and I didn't tell her I made first class. One day I came home in my uniform, and I had my new first-class crow on while I was sitting around the house.* So she was wondering when I was going to take my uniform off. [Laughter]

Q: You were wondering when she'd notice.

Master Chief Brashear: Oh, yes, but she never did notice it until I finally told her. I said, "I made first class." Boy, she was excited. Pay got up to $230.00 a month.

Q: Big time.

Master Chief Brashear: Big time, yes, $230.00 a month. We lived on 126th Street during those days, and my first son was born there on 126th Street. Then we moved to Long Island, and in 1956 I had my first tour of shore duty, in Rhode Island.

Q: Please tell me about that.

Master Chief Brashear: Well, I went to Quonset Point, Rhode Island, as a first class boatswain's mate, and I was in charge. I was the leading petty officer at the boat house and, of course, for diving. That was a two-year shore duty. During those two years, I picked up a lot of dead people and a lot of airplanes, including one Blue Angel.† So the job up there consisted of picking up the airplanes that had crashed and running those boats. At the

---

* "Crow" is the nickname for the sewn-on design of an eagle that appears as part of a petty officer's rating badge. The nickname is particulary apt when a sailor is wearing his white uniform. In that case, the eagle is a dark blue, nearly black.
† The Navy's flight demonstration team is known as the Blue Angels.

Quonset Point Naval Air Station, one of the planes they had was the AD type.[*] Well, when the ADs would come around and come in and approach runway 16, they had to come between two huge buildings. This one guy figured out and said when those airplanes went between those two buildings and then when they got on the other side, the air turbulence was causing them to crash. I don't know if there was anything to it or not, but I sure picked up a lot of airplanes.

Q: Could be. Did you enjoy that tour of duty?

Master Chief Brashear: Yes, I did. And during that tour of duty, I got a letter that I would be assigned with President Eisenhower.[†] So I went with Eisenhower for about 180 days out of that tour of duty.

Q: You weren't stationed at the White House, were you?

Master Chief Brashear: No. No. When he would come to Rhode Island to play golf at Newport, I would take the 104-foot crash boat and meet the Barbara Ann at Delaware and escort it to Rhode Island.[‡] During the whole time he would be there, I would escort the Barbara Ann. I would carry Jim Hagerty and Secret Service people and what have you.[§] One time Mamie rode with me when I escorted the Barbara Ann.[**]

Q: What was the purpose of that, just safety?

---

[*] The Douglas AD Skyraider was one of the Navy's primary carrier-based attack planes of the period.
[†] Dwight D. Eisenhower served as President of the United States from January 1953 to January 1961.
[‡] Barbara Ann was the name of a presidential yacht.
[§] James Hagerty was the President's press secretary.
[**] Mamie Eisenhower was the President's wife.

Master Chief Brashear: Yes. Everywhere the Barbara Ann went, I went. When they'd go out on a moonlight cruise, I'd escort it. I would escort the Barbara Ann until late in the evening, until he went to his cabin, and then I could secure it and go back over. He made a lot of trips up there.

Q: It sounds like pleasant duty.

Master Chief Brashear: A lot of trips. I was very fortunate that I got picked for the job. Somewhere one day I asked Jim Hagerty how he knew who I was when he came aboard my boat. He told me, "Son, we knew you long before we got there." [Laughter]

Q: I'll bet you had been checked out.

Master Chief Brashear: Yes.

Q: Did you get to meet the President?

Master Chief Brashear: Yes, I met the President. He didn't talk to me as much as Mamie. Mamie talked to me about three or four times a week. But Ike didn't talk to me but about, maybe, once a week. But when I left, he gave me a little knife that said, "To Carl M. Brashear. From Dwight D. Eisenhower, 1957. Many, many thanks." And then I got an invitation to go to his funeral too.

Q: What impressions do you have of Eisenhower from your meetings? Was he friendly?

Master Chief Brashear: Yes, he was very friendly. He wasn't as friendly as Mamie. Mamie called me "Son." All the time she called me "Son." Every time, "Son, Son." And the skipper of the Barbara Ann asked me to request to be assigned to their staff and they'd make me an ensign. Now, let me rephrase that. He said I'd have good chance to get a commission if I was on their staff. But I had to turn that down, because my goal was to make chief and to become the first black master diver in the Navy.

Q: Well, that was an attractive offer, nonetheless.

Master Chief Brashear: It certainly was, yep. During my tour with him, and when he'd come up there, I'd be around with all those guys, especially Jim Hagerty. He was a pistol.

Q: What do you remember about him?

Master Chief Brashear: Well, what I remember most vividly about Jim Hagerty, we went to Block Island, and we were to map a tour for the President. Well, to get into Block Island, it was very close. Then I had to twist the boat around and back it in, see, because you couldn't pull in. You had to be ready to leave, see.

So Jim Hagerty said, "Let me run your boat there, Brashear."

I said, "Okay." So I showed him the controls and showed him how to give orders down to the doggone people in the engine room and everything. He floundered around out there for about 10 or 15 minutes, and he hadn't done a thing.

He said, "I guess you better take it."

I said, "Yeah, I think so too." [Laughter]

Q: So you became a pretty good skipper?

Master Chief Brashear: Oh, yes, I was good. I was a good skipper. I'd run the boat down to Brooklyn and Long Island, independently steaming and with my crew.

Q: How big a crew did you have?

Master Chief Brashear: I had 13 people, two 20-millimeter guns on each wing of the bridge.

Q: Did you have any Secret Service people along on your boat?

Master Chief Brashear: Most of the time I had Secret Service and Jim Hagerty. But I have run independently, just my crew and I, to Brooklyn and Long Island, places like that.

Q: What else do you remember about the tour at Newport?

Master Chief Brashear: Well, one of my sons was born up there. That's what I remember mostly. My number-two son was born in North Cranston in Rhode Island. But I pretty well summed it up, I guess, about Newport. It was a two-year tour of duty there, and, as I said before, we just had a lot of airplane crashes during those days and during the two years that I was there and escorting the Barbara Ann.

Q: Do you know how you came to be picked for that escort role?

Master Chief Brashear: Not truthfully. I really don't know how I was picked for it, because we had three first-class boatswain's mates there at the boat house and quite a few first-class boatswain's mates on the station. I don't know how I was picked for that, but when I was a second-class boatswain's mate and won "sailor of the year," that's when they started calling me "Mr. Navy." It could have been something down through the years that caught the eye of somebody. I really don't know.

Q: Well, that award may well have had something to do with it.

Master Chief Brashear: Could have. Could have. And I was always a physically fit, well-proportioned sailor. I took a lot of pride in my uniforms, took a lot of pride in my appearance--peculiar sometimes, I guess. I'd be on the ship and on some dirty job like the one I had this morning. Well, before I'd go back to work in the afternoon, I'd have on a clean set of dungarees. I was always sort of a nut for looking sharp.

Q: The Navy puts a lot of emphasis on appearance, so that undoubtedly helped.

Master Chief Brashear: Yes, I always took a lot of pride in my appearance. Right now I do the same thing. But I don't really truthfully know how I got selected to be with Eisenhower. It was a good thing to happen to me, though.

Q: Where did you go from Quonset?

Master Chief Brashear: From Quonset Port, Rhode Island, I went to a ship repair facility in Guam. And there I stayed two years in a diving job with the exception of about seven months of that TAD on an ATA that belonged to the ship repair facility.[*] During this tour of duty, we did a lot of underwater work on destroyers and a lot of demolition work. We blasted out a channel while I was on board going into a place called Merizo, which was a Loran station during those days.[†] We shot something like 60,000 pounds of explosives to deepen this channel 3 feet to 15 feet so they could get a fuel barge in. Sometimes we would shoot electric; sometimes we'd fire non-electric.

On one particular day, we had a 500-pound bomb that we had rolled under a coral head, and theoretically, if you fire non-electric, it would have to go off--no other way, it would have to explode. So we set our charge and pulled the igniter. Then I held it to my ear, hearing it burn. Then we'd go in to the beach and wait for it to explode. It never went off. Now, this was supposed to have been impossible. So now what were we going to do? So we gave it another 30 minutes, another 30 minutes, another 30 minutes. We said, "Well, we've got to go check it." Stillwell, just as we were getting into the boat, that 500-pound bomb went off.

Q: How far away from it were you?

---

[*] ATA--auxiliary ocean tug.
[†] Loran (long-range aid to navigation) is a system of electronic navigation that involves the reception of pulse signals transmitted simultaneously by paired stations ashore.

Master Chief Brashear: We were quite a ways from it, but she went off. But if it had been 15 more minutes, we'd have been right on top of it. We did not know how that happened. Our commanding officer wrote letters, wrote letters, and wrote letters back to EDU and EOD.* He wrote everybody. The feedback we got said that we must have messed up on timing the safety fuze or we did this, you know. But we didn't. And that was a close call, very close. But we got a lot of demolition experience the two years that I was on Guam.

Q: What other examples do you remember?

Master Chief Brashear: I remember a lot of people getting hurt on Guam diving. There was good sports diving down in Guam, and everybody wanted a set of scuba gear to go sports diving.† One Sunday morning this one lieutenant named White was diving, and I guess he embolized himself. He never did walk after that--Lieutenant (j.g.) White. I never will forget that man's name. We treated him there at the ship repair facility in the hyperbaric chamber. We got him back to the surface, and he still couldn't walk.

Q: Did you take up scuba diving yourself?

Master Chief Brashear: Oh, yes, but I trained as a Navy scuba diver.

Q: When did you learn that in addition to the deep-sea diving?

Master Chief Brashear: We phased in scuba in '56 and '57. I got about three weeks of it while I was in Rhode Island, and we phased in with the Scott hydropack. We had that.

Q: I'm not familiar with that.

---

* EDU and EOD--experimental diving unit, explosive ordnance disposal.
† Scuba--self-contained underwater breathing apparatus.

Master Chief Brashear: Okay. If we had a first-class diver, the Navy authorized him to train us to phase in for us to be scuba, and then we got scuba designation along with being a regular diver. So I got mine about '56, '57.

Q: What are the advantages of that over the rig you'd been using?

Master Chief Brashear: Mobility. Depth control. Freedom of movement. That's scuba over deep sea or the cumbersome diving suit. Quick jobs. During those days, you could dive to 60 feet in scuba; now you can dive to 130.

Q: Did you still need tenders? How did that work?

Master Chief Brashear: No, you don't need a tender if you dive with a buddy. You don't have to be tethered. If you dive in the buddy system, you would just keep contact with your buddy. Now, you're never supposed to dive in scuba without a buddy system. But if a case does happen, then you're supposed to be tethered, a tender line, but just in extreme emergency cases.

Q: How was the water out there in Guam? Could you see fairly well?

Master Chief Brashear: Yards and yards. Visibility was tremendous. As a matter of fact, when you go out there and dive and come back to the East Coast and the lights go out, it makes you think about, "Do I want to continue in this field or not?" [Laughter]

Q: You get spoiled.

Master Chief Brashear: You get spoiled out there diving in that kind of weather. When you were working on the bottom and dropped a nut, you just said, "Well, I'll put all these on, and I'll reach down and get it." The white coral was just tremendous. You can see a lot.

Q: So then was it a case that you used the deep-sea rig only if you were going deeper than 130 feet?

Master Chief Brashear: Yes. Or if it was inside of a wreck, you use the deep-sea gear. You cannot go inside of a wreck with scuba gear because you don't have a free ascent back to the surface. So you have to use your deep-sea gear or if it's over 130 feet.

Q: What was Guam like as a place for your family?

Master Chief Brashear: Very nice. Very nice. Not a lot of clothes. A lot of recreation. It was just a very nice place to have a family. I liked it so well out there that I put in for a year's extension, and it was approved. So that would give me three years on Guam. I took the exam for chief and made it in about 1959. I put my new uniform on in '60, and they canceled my extension.

Q: Oh, no.

Master Chief Brashear: That's right. So I said, "By God! You make chief, and it's a disadvantage." So then I had to buy all those winter clothes and come back to the States. But that's where I made chief.

Q: Were your children old enough to be in school out there?

Master Chief Brashear: No. No. My first son was born in '55 in New York, so he was only two or three years old. My other guy was born in Rhode Island. I only had the two, and they were very young.

Q: What are some of the other jobs you remember from that tour of duty?

Master Chief Brashear: Well, I remember jobs in Truk Island.* We had to blast out an LST ramp at Truk, and the mosquitoes were so big that they'd eat you alive. I think they'd argue and say, "Which one's going to take him now?" [Laughter] Those were the biggest mosquitoes I believe I've ever seen in my life. We had those nets around us, you know, and you could feel it against that net, seemed like he was trying to get through that. Those were huge mosquitoes. I remember that job at Truk Island.

In order to dive there and get the reef to blow right off the water, we had to run the jackhammer under the water, see. So we had a compressor in a boat this time and a face mask. Then the guy was holding me down so I could get my jackhammer so I could get my explosives inside this rock. I turned the jackhammer loose and knocked my mask off, and he didn't know my mask was off. So he was still holding me down, and I'm pushing him trying to get his attention. I didn't have any air, see. [Laughter] So he thought that I was just trying to stay down. But the jackhammer knocked my mask off, and I had a heck of a time getting his attention to tell him I didn't have my mask on. He finally turned me loose where I could come to get some gas.

Q: How long did that last without air?

Master Chief Brashear: Oh, just a few seconds, but it seemed like it was forever.

Q: I'll bet.

Master Chief Brashear: Because, see, he was holding me down so I could get leverage with this jackhammer. But when I slipped and the jackhammer hit my mask and knocked it off, he didn't know it. So he was holding me just a few seconds.

Q: What other jobs do you remember?

---

* The Truk Islands are a group in the central Caroline chain in the Central Pacific. Truk was the site of a major Japanese naval base during World War II.

Master Chief Brashear: That was about the extent of Guam. I think we dove five and six days a week and a lot of demolition work.

One time we had a job up in Chichi Jima.[*] So this time I went TAD on the ship repair facility's ATA. We bummed us a master diver. We had one master diver that they flew down there. So he got his diving team together, and I was part of the diving team. So we went to Chichi Jima on the ATA to hook up a mooring buoy. A cruiser had broken the riser chain, and then the ground ring fell to the bottom. Well, we went up there to try to find those legs to this moor. We were diving on an old gasoline Leroy compressor. After a while our loofa sponges got all oily, greasy, couldn't find any loofa sponges. Chichi Jima has about 16 families living on it, a little old small commissary.

So Chief French told me, "Get in the boat and go to the commissary and buy all the Kotex you can find."

I said, "Come on, Chief. You know I'm not going over there and buy any Kotex."

He said, "Yes, you are too."

I was the first class boatswain's mate, and he was the chief, see. So I got in the boat and went over there to the commissary, and I tried to hang around the commissary until there wasn't anybody in it. But every time I'd look in there, people were in the commissary. So I went into the little exchange off the side, and I got those boxes of Kotex to put in place of our loofa sponges. I brought them back to the ship and put them in there. So that night we went up to the little club they had, and the word had got around that we had come in that store and bought some Kotex. [Laughter] They were wondering what that ship is doing out there buying Kotex.

Q: It would make people wonder.

---

[*] Chichi Jima is in the Bonin Islands, near Japan. One of the other islands in the group is Iwo Jima.

Master Chief Brashear: They were talking about us. But there again, we weren't even thinking about safety. We stuffed those Kotex in this oil separator. And they worked. [Laughter]

Q: Well, they're absorbent.

Master Chief Brashear: Yes. So then we finally found the ground ring, and the ground ring was about 16 feet from the chain that was going down, about 2-1/2 inch chain now. So I went down. Chief French thought I was the best diver in the world. I went down in a deep-sea suit and ran a 5/8-inch wire through this ground ring. And just imagine yourself, visibility is good. I looked up and saw the riser chain coming down, and I was in a deep-sea suit and used a controlled blowup to this riser chain. Then I hooked this 5/8-inch wire about five or six links up this riser chain. I told them on the ship to heave around on the 5/8-inch wire with the winch. So this brought the ground ring up. You could see the big rings. This brought it up to the link. I put a detachable link in there by myself and put it together and put the lead in it.

Q: Now, was this on deck or still underwater?

Master Chief Brashear: No, 80-some feet of water. Yes, sir. Can you imagine what we had to do?

Q: Yes, I can imagine it.

Master Chief Brashear: Put that through the ground ring and about four or five links up the riser chain I put a choker around it, and then when they heaved around on the ship, that brought the ring up to the riser chain.

Q: I understand now.

Master Chief Brashear: And I put the detachable link in it and hooked it up.

Q: So you had to be a boatswain's mate as well as a diver to be able to pull that off.

Master Chief Brashear: Yes, sir. I thought that was very unique to be able to use a controlled blowup and tenders helping you and hold yourself there, you know, you just put a hook around you diving. That was illegal, too, but I stayed there and put that detachable link in that doggone chain.

Q: How did you keep yourself at a certain depth like that to do the work?

Master Chief Brashear: Well, see, once I blew myself up there, I fastened myself to that chain. But I wasn't supposed to do that. If something happened to me, they couldn't pull me up. I was just taking that chance. I made myself heavy, and I hung there. When they pulled the riser chain up to me, then I put my detachable link in.

Q: Now, how did you blow yourself up to it?

Master Chief Brashear: Now, the way I blew myself from off the bottom to about 15 feet up this riser chain, I pulled in on my chin button and not let any air out, and it would just inflate my suit. Well, I had ahold of my 5/8-inch wire, and I'd just give myself a little slack, just blow it up, you know, and just slacking myself off. [Laughter] It takes a lot of know-how.

Q: You have to know what you're doing.

Master Chief Brashear: Oh, yes, you do. Yes, you do. If I would have lost control and blown from 80-some feet back to the surface and hit up under that buoy or hit up under the ship, I'd be killed.

Q: Not to mention the bends even if you hadn't run into something.

Master Chief Brashear: The suit could have ruptured, and I'd get upside down and fall back and drown. It just takes a lot of know-how.

Q: Well, you said you wound up that tour in Guam. Where did you go from there?

Master Chief Brashear: I left Guam and went aboard the USS Nereus in San Diego, California, a short stop there, and then on to first-class diver school in Washington, D.C. I got to Washington, D.C., in 1960. The stay was short. I flunked out of first class. Blew it. Stillwell, every salvage diver that went to that school as a salvage diver and flunked out of first-class school left as a second-class diver. Many of them had flunked out. First-class school was a hard school, very hard.

Q: In what ways?

Master Chief Brashear: Physics. Medicine. Decompression. Treatments. Ratio proportion, mixing gases to the proper ratio. Very hard and just a lot of math. I mean, God, it was hard! Flunked it. They called me in and told me, said, "You're leaving as a non-diver." I could have gone through the floor. I'd been diving for seven years and left as a non-diver, went back aboard the Nereus and had to show up there as a non-diver, chief petty officer. So I stayed there for a short period. I said, "I've got to get off of this ship."

Q: That was probably the lowest point in your career.

Master Chief Brashear: Man, I hit rock bottom. I said, "I've got to get off of this ship." So I got a set of orders to the fleet training center in Hawaii. I went there as the chief master-at-arms, non-diver, just regular chief boatswain's mate. A second-class diving school was in Hawaii, also. They had a school there, and the man in charge of that school was Billie

Delanoy.* I knew Billie when he was much younger.†

I called him, and I said, "Billie, "I'm over here at the fleet training center."

He said, "What the fuck you doing at the fleet training center, Brash?"

I said, "I'm over here in the chief master-at-arms billet."

He said, "You always could lie good." But I convinced him I was over there to the fleet training center as chief master-at-arms. He said, "Come over here and see me." So I went to see him. And he said, "Well, shoot. You got to be on a diving billet."

I said, "Bill, I'm not a diver." Of course, we got into the details that I had gone to first-class school and flunked out and left as a non-diver. He hit the overhead.

So he saw my executive officer, and I went to second-class school from the fleet training center, graduated as a second-class diver, back from a salvage diver to a second-class diver to graduate.

Q: What were some of the things you learned in that school that helped you?

Master Chief Brashear: Nothing. Because second-class school you don't have much on physics and medicine and gases. All I was doing was just getting back to being a second-class diver. That's below a salvage diver. Didn't learn anything. All I had to do there was show up and be there to get my diploma. I got my diploma and came back to the fleet training center.

Q: When the tape recorder wasn't running, Master Chief, you mentioned to me that you had done some diving on the hull of the Arizona when you were out in Hawaii.‡

---

* Lieutenant (junior grade) Billie L. Delanoy, USN. He was a former enlisted man then serving as a limited duty officer.
† Delanoy was born in 1928, about three years before Brashear.
‡ The battleship Arizona (BB-39) was commissioned in 1916. On 7 December 1941, while moored in Pearl Harbor, she was hit by a Japanese bomb that created a tremendous magazine explosion. The ship burned for three days; all told 1,177 of her crewmen were killed. In the 1950s the Navy erected a temporary memorial over the hull. In 1962 it completed a permanent memorial that has become a popular tourist attraction for visitors to Hawaii.

Master Chief Brashear: I recall diving on the Arizona the last of '61 and early '62 to determine how much of a list she had. This was prior to putting a memorial on it. Of all the diving I did in my time, this gave me a different feeling. I got down and thought about those 1,100 shipmates down there that didn't make it out. It seemed like it was a different atmosphere, a different experience. You get a different feeling diving on the Arizona than you did any other place.

Q: How would you describe that feeling?

Master Chief Brashear: It's hard to describe how you feel, Stillwell. It just seems like your bubbles coming out of your scuba gear were making a lot of noise. Seems like when you touch the ship it just make a lot of noise.

Q: Was it an eerie feeling?

Master Chief Brashear: It was just an eerie feeling to be down there, yes, it was.

Q: Did you get a chance to look in any portholes and see the inside of the ship?

Master Chief Brashear: No. No, I didn't get a chance to look in any portholes. Where they took the 14-inch guns off on the forward mount, you could see a big hole there, but you couldn't see anything down in it.

Q: What did you determine from your survey?

Master Chief Brashear: We determined that she had about almost a two-degree list on it. When the bomb went down into the hull, it looked like it just blew a hole in the bottom of it, and she just sat right on the bottom. At low tide, the bitts and the lifeline are out of the water. And from time to time, at that time, you could see little bubbles of oil coming to the surface.

Q: How did you measure this two-degree list?

Master Chief Brashear: We took plumb lines, and every three or four feet we would measure from the weather deck to the mud around the ship.

Q: How would that degree of list affect the building of a memorial?

Master Chief Brashear: Well, now, I'm not an architect, so I really don't know. [Laughter] But I guess they had to erect it when they put the pillars or the stage under the memorial to hold it up, they'd have to be different lengths, because, see, she's resting on the main deck, with so many feet of it exposed on either side of the main deck. So I guess they'd have to build up to make the memorial level according to the list.

Q: Well, she's a special ship, so it's appropriate that you would get a special feeling.

Master Chief Brashear: Yes. You certainly did. And just, as you say, it was an eerie feeling, 1,100 of these shipmates in there. Yes.

Q: What was your next duty?

Master Chief Brashear: While I was still at the fleet training center, I got TAD orders and went to Joint Task Force Eight as a diver for nuclear testing. I did my 180 days there at Joint Task Force Eight on Johnston Island and Christmas Island, testing those nuclear bombs.[*]

---

[*] This testing took place in 1962 as part of Operation Dominic. On 25 April 1962, Joint Task Force Eight conducted the first U.S. atmospheric nuclear weapons test since 1958.

Q: Please tell me more about that joint task force and your work there.

Master Chief Brashear: Well, we went to Joint Task Force Eight to test the Thor missiles.* That was on Johnston Island. So I went down there as a diver and in charge of a YTB.† I ran YTB-262 while I was there. I called it "Surf Side 262." There was an old TV program called "Surf Side Two Six [whatever]," so that's what I named it.

I was there as a tug skipper and as a diver. I was recommended for the Joint Service Medal and got it. General Starbird was our commanding officer, an Army general, and he talked to me one time for about a half a day it seemed like.‡ He busted my first class engineman, my chief engineer. He busted him. We were sitting there one night on the boat drinking beer. Well, the facilities were too small to accommodate us on Johnston Island when they set up this joint task force. So General Starbird said that everybody could drink beer on their crafts, but they had to control it.

So we were sitting there drinking beer one night, and a first-class engineman named Meyers said he was going to go up and fire the missile. I thought he was kidding. The boat skipper and the chief engineer had bikes. So he got on his bike, and, hell, I thought he was just shooting the breeze, you know. Before you know it, here came security down to my boat and cornered me. They had him locked up in a little old makeshift brig they had up there and put him on report for trying to get through the security to shoot the Thor missile. The Thor missile was on the launching pad, big lights around, with the liquid oxygen coming all around that booger. Pretty thing. Man, it was pretty. And he got busted from that, and then General Starbird called me up and talked to me about it. Meyers said that a general couldn't bust him, but he did.

Q: Found out he could.

---

* Thor was a U.S. Air Force single-stage, liquid-fueled, intermediate-range (1,650 miles) ballistic missile. It was designed as a stopgap to provide an interim nuclear capability while the United States developed the first large intercontinental ballistic missiles. It was first tested in 1957 and served into the early 1960s.
† YTB--large self-propelled harbor tug.
‡ Major General Alfred D. Starbird, USA, was Commander Joint Task Force Eight.

Master Chief Brashear: Yes, threw him off the island. He was on the plane after the general held office hours on him, they call it. He was gone on the plane the next day, and I didn't have a chief engineer. I had to use my fireman to run my boat. So that was an exciting tour, watching them shoot the Thor missile. So we finished that test on Johnston Island.

Q: What kind of a role was there for divers and a YTB in that testing environment?

Master Chief Brashear: Well, the YTB was there to bring the barges and equipment down the little channel that the big ships couldn't get in. You know, we'd go out and get a barge and bring in supplies and equipment to Johnston Island.

Q: Did it require any diving in that job?

Master Chief Brashear: I never made but one dive while I was there, and it was to check the screws on one of the small boats.

Q: So this was more of a boatswain's mate job.

Chief Brashear: Right, this was more of a boatswain's mate job. But we had four divers attached to Joint Task Force Eight, just to be there. So we finished up the Thor, shooting the missiles on Johnston. We sent the YTB back to the States. I didn't drive it back to the States. Another guy took it back to Hawaii for me. I got an LCU.* I was a skipper of an LCU, and went to Christmas Island, shooting the high-altitude bombs over there. We stayed there for the duration of the nuclear testing. But when I took command of the LCU, I put it in the Cabildo to take it around from Johnston Island to Christmas Island.† So if

---

* LCU--landing craft utility.
† The USS Cabildo (LSD-16) was a dock landing ship with a well deck at the stern that could flood down to let landing craft enter.

you're ever on Johnston Island, you know how those swells are out there, swells going up and down. So the first approach I made to the Cabildo, they hauled up bravo, so I had to move. You know, when they haul up the bravo flag, boats can't come in.*

I made about two approaches at the Cabildo. I said, "Well, I'm going in this time whether they haul that flag up there or not." [Laughter] So the exec was standing up on the bridge. You can just visualize this. Now, the Cabildo was flooded down, and I was going to run an LCU into it. Just as she went down, I passed over the sill doing standard. Now, you're only supposed to go in there at one-third speed. I passed over the sill doing standard and backed down full on those three engines. The forward part of the ship's well deck, the far bulkhead, was coming to me so fast. It looked like I was trying to stop my own ship, you know, pulling back up. I was backing down full inside that well deck, and that was churning up that water. The exec sent the boatswain down there and said, "You tell that fool he's crazy!" But I got it in there.

So I was skipper of the LCU-1459 when we took it around to Johnston Island, and I stayed on that until we finished up the nuclear testing. Now, we had a bet with ourselves. We had three LCUs there with three chief boatswain's mates. We had a dog leg in the little old channel to go out to the ships and load our LCUs up and bring back in the supplies.

Q: Was this at Christmas or Johnston?

Master Chief Brashear: This was Christmas. Couldn't use the YTB at Christmas. So Bulldog Thurman was there for this deep, deep explosive moor. That's the same guy I was talking about at the diving school in Bayonne, New Jersey. So we got permission from Bulldog Thurman to back one of those LCUs all the way through that channel. We

---

* The red "bravo" flag, signifying the letter B in the phonetic alphabet, warns of dangerous conditions.

were not supposed to do this because of the wind and the current. If you couldn't make it, you were supposed to turn around, and then Bulldog Thurman would tell you that you weren't a good chief boatswain's mate. Did you know that I backed that LCU one mile and a quarter. I backed it all the way back into the pier without ever turning around. That was winding up Christmas Island.

Q: Was there any concern about radiation during those tests?

Master Chief Brashear: Yes. Film badges would read a little high, you know, and a couple of guys had to leave the island a couple of times.

Q: Well, this sounds like a very exciting thing. It must have appealed to your sense of adventure.

Master Chief Brashear: Yes, it was exciting watching those high-altitude bombs go off and working around that.

Q: What is it like to see when it went off?

Master Chief Brashear: Well, let's talk about the Thor missile first.

Q: All right.

Master Chief Brashear: When they shot the Thor missile at Christmas Island, my wife took pictures at Hawaii just like daylight. And that was what it was like on Johnston Island, just like day. The high-altitude bombs on Christmas Island--oh, my God! That was a fireball up there! And the aftershock. You'd have to get in a kneeling position and be under this tent. You knew that this could just shock you.

Q: You couldn't look at it, could you?

Master Chief Brashear: No, you couldn't look at it. No. But when they'd shoot one of those 20- or 30-megaton bombs, it would rock that island.

Q: How high was the altitude? Do you recall?

Master Chief Brashear: I've forgotten now how high it was.

Q: What was the purpose of firing them so high?

Master Chief Brashear: Well, that I don't know. I really don't know what the purpose was. I couldn't answer that. I wasn't into that phase of it. I'd have to ask Admiral Mustin. Now, he was the admiral in charge of that one.[*]

Admiral Mustin got angry at the chiefs. We had good recreation on Christmas Island, which we didn't have on Johnston. So we'd have fishing parties quite frequently, but he never did catch as big a fish as the chiefs. So he said, "Those chiefs have got something together." But he never did catch a fish like we did.

Q: What kind of a guy was he like to work with?

Master Chief Brashear: Very nice, very nice. Good man.

Q: Very intelligent too.

---

[*] Rear Admiral Lloyd C. Mustin, USN. The oral history of Mustin, who retired as a vice admiral, is in the Naval Institute collection.

Master Chief Brashear: Yes, yes. I had him on my boat a lot of times, going out to the ships. Very nice guy. So we completed and came back to Hawaii. By then, I had PCS orders to the USS Coucal.*

Q: What do you remember about your duty on board her?

Master Chief Brashear: Lot of hard work with the four-point moors, training for rescuing personnel out of a submarine and just preparing myself for first-class school and going to sea a lot, making the WestPac cruises.†

Q: Where was she homeported?

Master Chief Brashear: Hawaii.

Q: Well, you probably got some good liberty there.

Master Chief Brashear: Yes. We had some good liberty in different ports. We went to Okinawa and the Philippines, Japan. Our skipper was Stenke.‡ He invented the Stenke hood. Did you ever hear of that?

Q: No, I'm not familiar with that.

---

* PCS--permanent change of station orders, which differed from the temporary additional duty orders Brashear had to Joint Task Force Eight. The submarine rescue ship Coucal (ASR-8) was commissioned 22 January 1943. Characteristics included displacement, 1,780 tons; length, 251 feet; beam, 42 feet; draft, 14 feet; top speed, 16.5 knots; armament, two 3-inch guns.
† WestPac--Western Pacific.
‡ Lieutenant George Stenke, USN.

Master Chief Brashear: The Stenke hood is used for making a buoyant ascent out of a submarine; you can breathe freely all the way to the surface. Instead of exhaling to the surface, you can breathe freely with the Stenke hood. He was the daddy of the Stenke hood, and I helped him quite a bit on it and worked with him. I've trained with it quite a bit since then.

Q: So it sounds as if that was entirely a training type experience on board that ship, because you didn't have any submarines to rescue.

Master Chief Brashear: Just really a training type, yes. We would take the submarine rescue chamber and fasten it to a submarine and drill at getting people out of the submarine. If we didn't have a submarine, we'd put the false seat on the bottom, just like a submarine hatch, and run our submarine rescue chamber up and down for training.

Q: Was this still the old McCann bell?

Master Chief Brashear: The McCann submarine rescue chamber. It paid for herself on the Squalus, so it's still around and will always be around.* I've forgotten the name of the skipper after Stenke, but he didn't want me to jack down the bell. I parted the down-haul cable, and when you take the bell down, you have 1,000 pounds of positive buoyancy. I broke the down-haul cable, and she came back to the surface. So they said, "The boatswain's mate's got too much muscle and no brains. Don't let him back." So we came

---

* The USS Squalus (SS-192), commanded by Lieutenant Oliver F. Naquin, USN, sank in 243 feet of water while conducting exercise dives on 23 May 1939 off Portsmouth, New Hampshire. Twenty-six men died, but 33, including Naquin, were recovered through the use of the McCann rescue chamber. The submarine later was salvaged, refurbished, and renamed the Sailfish. For details, see Carl La VO, Back from the Deep (Annapolis; Naval Institute Press, 1994).

back to the surface with 1,000 pounds of positive buoyancy, just rolling around on the surface.

Q: How deep could you go with that capability?

Master Chief Brashear: About 900 feet. The down-haul cable is 1,100, so you always keep a little bit on the deck to play with. So between 900 and 950 feet is about the best you can go with the McCann.

Q: How often would you get a submarine to work with in a situation like that?

Master Chief Brashear: Quite frequently. You'd be amazed at how those people like to go out and train and get in that bell and come back to the surface.

Q: It could be their lives at stake.

Master Chief Brashear: Yes, right, right. And you've always got a few on the submarine that are anxious to get out of the submarine and get in the bell. So they stand right under the hatch waiting for you to open it. You know they're there, so you like to open it quick and get them wet, see. [Laughter]

I'd like to tell you a little story about what happened to me on the <u>Coucal</u>. The submarine squadron commander came down and inspected the ship. During the critique, he made a statement in the wardroom that the boatswain and I kept everything locked up. He said, "Everywhere I looked, there was a goody locker. They've got nice brooms, nice swabs. But whenever I saw somebody sweeping, it was with a worn-out broom." He just talked about me and the boatswain pretty bad during the critique. I guess he just had a thing about cleaning gear.

The ship was going to WestPac, and he would always come down and see the ships off and say goodbye to the commanding officer. So I got an old greasy broom from the engine room and wrapped it up in a nice box and presented it to him on the quarterdeck. So I gave him this present for being so nice and everything. The ship hadn't even gotten outside the buoys when we got a message. This is making it short, but he put it in words that said, "You better be glad I'll be relieved before you get back." [Laughter] I had to do something to get back with him for talking about our brooms.

Q: I bet your skipper wasn't too glad you did that.

Master Chief Brashear: Oh, yes, he was.

Q: Oh, he was in on it?

Master Chief Brashear: Oh, sure. It was a gimmick, and he was in on it. And the squadron commander was sending back a gimmick, too, when he said, "You better be glad I'll be relieved before you get back."

Q: So he wasn't really mad.

Master Chief Brashear: Oh, no, no, no.

Q: What else do you remember about that ship?

Master Chief Brashear: It was a good tour of duty. That's what I remember about it. I learned a lot on there. We had a master diver on there named Flanagan, and if I'd get hung up on working out a formula to mix gases, he would help me prepare myself for first-class school.* One day I said to him, "Pat, I have to go to first-class school."

He said, "Yeah, you're right. You've got to go." He said, "We've known a long time, you've got to go."

Stillwell, I studied math from 1961 to 1963, day and night. Got a set of orders to go to the first-class diving school in Washington, D.C. Now, I'm reporting into the school with the attitude that, "Hey, I'm a salvage diver. I only have to go 14 weeks like the rest of the salvage divers and just get the mixed gas, physics and medicine and split and mixing and analyzing."

The training officer come and told me, he said, "Come on up here, Brash. Let me talk to you." So I went and talked to him. He said, "You know how long you're going to be here?"

I said, "Yeah, 14, 16 weeks. Whatever it takes for me to cross train."

He said, "No, you're not." He said, "You're going to be here 26." He made me go through the complete school just like I'd never been a salvage diver. I went through 26 weeks of school.

I said, "Well, okay. I'll just graduate out of this booger as number one." I was doing all right. I was making progress to graduate number one. We had a Korean with us, and the Korean was about to flunk out. So they wanted him to be with me on a lot of his work, for me to guide him along. They just almost told me I wasn't going to graduate number one, but they wanted me to help him. So I helped him to get him along, and I graduated number three.

Q: Out of how many?

Master Chief Brashear: We had 17 graduate out of that class.

---

* Chief Damage Controlman Patrick Flanagan, USN.

Q: Well, you did a lot better than the first school you went to.

Master Chief Brashear: Yes. Graduated number three out of a class of 17. Well, we started with 30. All the classes start with 30-some people.

Q: Did the Korean make it?

Master Chief Brashear: Yes, he made it.

Q: Great.

Master Chief Brashear: But they knew I was sharp in diving, and they knew I knew, and so they put me with him.

Q: Obviously you had learned what you needed to know in the meantime to pass the course.

Master Chief Brashear: Oh, yes. I would just drop the math part of it.

Q: Well, you had the motivation to do that.

Q: I've seen pictures of ARSs and ASRs, and they look pretty similar. What are the differences?

Master Chief Brashear: ASR is a submarine rescue ship equipped with the McCann rescue chamber, and an ARS is rescue and salvage equipped with salvage equipment and beach gear. That's the difference. So an ASR is equipped to dive with mixed gas, helium and oxygen. An ARS was equipped to dive with air--until they got the new ones.

Q: Just strictly a difference in function.

Master Chief Brashear: Yes. You had the mixed-gas capabilities on the ASR. That was a good training for me, too, because I'd never been on an ASR prior to going to first-class school the first time.

Q: Why do you have mixed gases as opposed to straight air?

Master Chief Brashear: Well, when you dive deeper than 300 feet, you have to have some kind of breathing medium to keep the mental and physical controlling center to form an artificial atmosphere, cut down on the nitrogen narcosis. They had done the research years and years ago and found that helium and oxygen mixed in the proper ratio was a good breathing medium for that purpose. Because, see, when you dive below 300 feet, you actually exceed the partial pressure of oxygen. So you would go into oxygen toxicity, oxygen poisoning. That's the reason you breathe helium and oxygen.

Q: I've heard this term "rapture of the deep." Did you ever have any experience with that?

Master Chief Brashear: Well, "rapture of the deep" is just like nitrogen narcosis. Every individual experiences that at four atmospheres or more; some are more severe than others.

Q: What are your memories of it? How does it affect you?

Master Chief Brashear: I didn't notice--and the instructors didn't notice--any nitrogen narcosis building up on me when we took our tests in deep-sea diving school. I didn't notice the four atmospheres. Now, on your initial training, they'll take you down to 287 feet in the chamber so the instructors can watch you. Everybody had a task to do at that 287 feet, to see which of those divers they had to be concerned the most in their training because of possible nitrogen narcosis.

While I was under that pressure, I figured my base pay for a year, and I wrote on the lines on the paper. Some people couldn't write on the lines. Some people couldn't take those pages and punch in the holes after a period of time. That was just how it affected them. I figured my base pay for a year and sat there and waited for those people to bring me back to the surface. Some guys would start laughing and couldn't stop. So nitrogen narcosis or "rapture of the deep" has different effects.

Q: Well, and apparently it's different physiology for different people too.

Master Chief Brashear: Yes. The physiology has quite a bit to do with it.

Q: Well, I guess you were just one of the lucky ones then for your line of work.

Master Chief Brashear: Yes. So, as I say, I noticed that my lips would feel like they had a little oil or something on them. But as far as I'm thinking, I don't notice it. On the deep dive, on the working dive up there, I saw a man one time, Stillwell, put a pin in a shackle, but he didn't have it in the wire. So that was just how it affected him.

Q: What kind of a compartment or a chamber were you in when they did this test?

Master Chief Brashear: Decompression chamber or recompression chamber. Now they call it the hyperbaric chamber; they gave it one name now. Of course, you have viewing ports, and you have the inner lock and the outer lock. So when they run this test, they open both locks and put enough people in there that they can watch through those three ports on this side and three ports on the other side. They have each person facing where that guy can sit there and watch you, you know. Each of us has a different task, and at 287 feet that's what you're supposed to do.

Q: Figure out your base pay.

Master Chief Brashear: Well, that was my task.

Q: I see.

Master Chief Brashear: To do my base pay per year rounded off. Other guys had to do other tasks.

Q: Was this in Washington?

Master Chief Brashear: This is in Washington, but they do the same thing down at Panama City, Florida, because they took the school down there.

Q: Anything else to mention about that time on the ASR before you went and passed the first-class diver's test?

Master Chief Brashear: We changed the screw on the Coucal a few times. We did it underwater. The guy that changed the screw with me the last time is a four-striper in the

Navy now. During that time, he was a first class MR, Billy Burke.* The last command he had was one of the LSTs out here at Little Creek. Back then he was second class diver, and I was the chief. So if he saw you today, he'd say, "Old Carl raised me good." [Laughter] Billy Burke is a good man, fantastic man.

When we changed the screw on the Coucal, we had the screw hanging down on a wire strap. So we said, "Well, we'll go to chow and put the screw on the shaft when we come back from chow." So while we were going to chow, I think the screw turned around. Right? So we went down to chainfall this booger into shape, you know, and we tried to put the small taper onto the shaft. It was on backwards. [Laughter] Boy, they laughed at us. They thought we were a couple of dummies.

There were some exciting times on there just being with the crew and working. And while I was there I picked up my OOD tactics and got my qualification for OOD.† As a chief boatswain's mate, I went to CIC team training, and I could handle the ship independently or in formation.

Q: You're a pretty versatile guy.

Master Chief Brashear: Yes. I was the only enlisted man on the ship who stood OOD watches under way, and I was command duty officer in port.

Q: Well, this was quite a change from being disrated as a diver to being back as a diver and officer of the deck as well.

Master Chief Brashear: Right.

---

* MR--machinery repairman.
† OOD--officer of the deck.

Q: What sort of duty did you have after you passed the first-class diver's test?

Master Chief Brashear: Okay. I went to first-class school and graduated number three. They didn't have a job on an ARS, so I went to an ATF, the USS Shakori.* You cannot get the proper qualification on an ATF to groom you for master, so I stayed on the Shakori for only one year.

Q: Why do you say you can't get the proper qualification?

Master Chief Brashear: Well, on something like that they mostly just tow. You don't do a lot of salvage jobs, because you just don't have the capabilities. So I stayed aboard there for a year and requested to go aboard the Hoist.†

Well, I got aboard the Hoist and was working and studying and preparing myself to be a master diver. This was when the accident happened and I tore my leg off.

Q: Please describe that.

Master Chief Brashear: Well, in 1966, the Air Force lost a nuclear bomb off the coast of Palomares, Spain.‡ The Air Force asked the Navy to recover that bomb, and, of course,

---

* The fleet ocean tug Shakori (ATF-162) was commissioned 20 December 1945. She was 205 feet long, 38 feet in the beam, had a draft of 15 feet, and a displacement of 1,675 tons. Her top speed was 16.5 knots.
† The salvage ship Hoist (ARS-40) was commissioned 21 July 1945. She was 214 feet long, 39 feet in the beam, had a draft of 14 feet, and a displacement of 1,360 tons. Her top speed was 15 knots.
‡ The collision of the two U.S. Air Force planes was on 17 January 1966. The bomb that fell into the sea near Palomares, Spain, was located by the U.S. Navy's deep-diving research vessel Alvin on 17 March. Once lines were attached to the bomb, it was brought to the surface on 7 April by the submarine rescue ship Petrel (ASR-14). The Hoist took part in the recovery operation.

the Navy said yes. Admiral Guest formed the task force, and we started searching for that bomb in January of 1966.*

The reason the bomb dropped in the water was that two airplanes were maneuvering, and the fuel plane was fueling a B-52. According to what the people said, it gained on the B-52 too fast, and they collided in midair. Three of the bombs' parachutes opened and landed over on the land in Spain. One of the parachutes didn't open, and it fell in the water. So we searched for the bomb close to the shoreline for about two and a half months, and all we were getting was pings on beer cans, coral heads, and other contacts.

Q: This is with your sonar?

Master Chief Brashear: Yes. But every time we would get a contact, we would dive on it. And we dove around the clock for two months. So the fisherman that saw the bomb go into the water kept telling the officials, "You're too close! Too close! Out there! Out there!" He'd take his fingers and measure. So one day Admiral Guest said we would try it. So they made a replica of the bomb on the tender and then dropped it to see how it would show up on the screen, same dimension, same length, same diameter. Then we went out six miles, and the first pass, there the bomb was, six miles in 2,600 feet of water.

So we rigged to pick this thing up. The CURV, out of Woods Hole was going down to hook this thing up.† Stillwell, I rigged up what I call a spider. It was a three-legged contraption that I was going to drop for this bomb to be hooked up to. I had my grapnel hooks and everything, you know. So the Hoist had a very good skipper. Doggone, he was nice!

We dropped that equipment in 2,600 feet of water, and it landed 15 feet from the bomb. The crew of Alvin said it was amazing. The parachute on the bomb hadn't opened,

---

* Rear Admiral William S. Guest, USN.
† CURV--controlled underwater recovery vehicle.

so the Alvin went down and put the parachute shrouds in the grapnel hooks that I had on each leg of the spider. But the Alvin ran out of batteries and had to surface.

So Admiral Guest, through the radio conversation with our skipper, said to pick it up. So we picked it up to a certain depth. Then we brought a boat alongside to pick the crate up out of the boat and set it on the deck to when I picked that bomb up I'd put it in this crate. I was picking the bomb up with the capstan. I got the crate, picking it up, and the boat broke loose. It was a Mike-8.[*] The engineer was revving up the engines, and it parted the line. I was trying to get my sailors out of the way, and I ran back down to grab a sailor, just manhandling him out of the way. Just as I started to leave, the boat pulled on the pipe that had the mooring line tied to it. That pipe came loose, flew across the deck, and it struck my leg below the knee. They said I was way up in the air just turning flips. I landed about two foot inside of that freeboard. They said if I'd been two feet farther over, I'd have gone over the side. I jumped up and started to run and fell over. That's when I knew how bad my leg was.[†]

Q: Was it taken off by the mooring line?

Master Chief Brashear: Taken off by a pipe and the boat's mooring line that parted.

Then we dropped the bomb back down into 2,600 feet of water. So there I was on the ship with my leg torn off--no doctor, no morphine, six and a half miles from the Albany. So the corpsmen placed two tourniquets on my leg. He was interviewed for a program in the "Comeback" TV series, and he said that the reason he couldn't stop the bleeding with two tourniquets was because I was in such good physical condition and my

---

[*] LCM-8, a particular model of the landing craft mechanized.
[†] The date of Chief Brashear's accident was 25 March 1966. The lower part of Brashear's leg was not torn off by the accident itself; instead he suffered compound fractures of both bones in the lower leg. A portion of his leg was amputated subsequently on 11 May 1966 because of persistent infection and necrosis.

leg was such a mass of muscle.

So we steamed towards the Albany. I was telling the guys about what I had rigged on the ship, and how to rerig it. Finally, we got to the Albany, which was just sitting there, but this little old ARS was just going up and down, up and down. So they just literally pitched me up onto the deck of the Albany, and I hit the deck. BOOM! I said, "Doggone, you didn't have to drop me that far." [Laughter]

Q: You were conscious this long?

Master Chief Brashear: Yes, I was still conscious. So I thought I was going to the sick bay on the Albany, but they put me in a helicopter towards Torrejon Air Force Base in Spain. They got the doctor off of the doggone cruiser. But they got in too big of a hurry. They didn't fuel the helicopter and couldn't make it. So they set me down on a dilapidated runway somewhere in Spain waiting for a two-engine small plane to come and get me and take me to Torrejon.

Well, the accident happened at 5:00 o'clock in the afternoon, and at 9:00 o'clock I was on the runway there. During this period of time before then, the doctor wouldn't give me any water. So I asked him for some water, and he said, "Well, you can have some." He told me this later. He said he was going to give it to me because I was going to die anyway. So he said, "Heck, I might as well give it to him. He's almost dead now."

Q: The tourniquets must have started working at some point. I mean, you couldn't bleed for four hours.

Master Chief Brashear: Oh, yes. I mean, they were doing a little, but weren't stopping it completely. I lost so much blood that I went into shock around 9:00 o'clock.

Q: I'm not surprised.

Master Chief Brashear: So then I just passed out. And I don't remember the plane coming to get me, or I don't remember getting into the hospital at Torrejon.

Now, I'm going to tell you some stuff that my doctor told me later in Torrejon. He said that when I was rolled into the emergency room at Torrejon Air Force Base, he said I didn't have any pulse whatsoever, no heartbeat, couldn't feel a thing, he said. But he said he told the medics to do something, but I can't recall what he said he told the medics to do. He said the medics were slow about doing it, and he said he thought he'd feel on me one more time. He said I had a very, very faint heartbeat, and that's when he found out I was alive. He said I almost was in the morgue. Right away, he started making fast arrangements to get some blood, and they pumped 18 pints of blood in me, and I came to.

Then they were going to piece my leg back on and do plastic surgery. Well, they were going to make my leg three inches shorter than the other leg. When they took the bandage off, my foot fell off. So they tried again, and it would fall off. It got gangrene and got infected. Well, I was slowly dying from that. So they transferred me up to Wiesbaden, Germany. There the doctor said that he could fix me, but it would take three years and could have me walking on a brace. So I raised all sorts of hell in that hospital.

So he said, "Well, do you want to be air-mailed out to the States?" That's the term he used. He said, "Do you want to be air-mailed out to the States?"

I said, "Yes, sir! Air-mail me out of here!"

So he air-mailed me to the States, and I arrived in McGuire Air Force Base.[*] I was there on the ward with other people that found out I was infected so bad, so then they carted me off out of there about midnight and put me in a little isolation place. That was McGuire.

---

[*] McGuire Air Force Base is adjacent to the Army's Fort Dix near Wrightstown, New Jersey.

So three days later, I came down to Portsmouth Naval Hospital.* Here again, Dr. O'Neill and an Air Force doctor--doggone, I can't remember his name now--but Dr. O'Neill was the major surgeon there.† He said he could have me fixed in 30 months or four years or something like that, have me walking on a brace. He told me all the different types of pins he could put on there. So I said, "Well, I can't stay here that long." I said, "I've got to get out of here." I said, "Go ahead and amputate."

So he said, "Geez, Chief! Anybody could amputate. It takes a good doctor to fix it."

I said, "Yeah, but I can't stay here three years. I can't be tied up that long. I've got to go back to diving." They just laughed, "The fool's crazy! He doesn't have the chance of a snowball in hell of staying in the Navy. And a diver? No way! Impossible!"

So they messed around with my leg so much and got it infected so bad I convinced them to go ahead and amputate. So they did a guillotine-type of operation, just chopped it off, cleared up the infection. A while later he said, "We didn't go high enough. We need to cut off another inch and a half." So they cut off an inch and a half to make sure they got it, and veed it out and sewed it up. This was in July 1966.

After that I kept saying, "I'm going to be a deep-sea diver, doggone it!" By this time, I was reading some books about a Canadian Air Force pilot that flew airplanes with no legs. I had also read books that said a prosthesis can support any amount of weight. I also read you've got to develop an attitude that, "Hey, look, I'm going to accept this. I'm going to make it work." I worked towards it.

So they got me good enough to go to Philadelphia to a prosthetic center to get a prosthesis. So I got up there, and they told me it would be about two months before they could fit me with a temporary cast to shrink my stump. And so I talked to them a little bit. About the next week after that I had a cast on my leg to shrink my stump, and I could walk with a cane. Then I said, "Well, I've got to start working out." I was feeling bad. So I was working out outside the hospital and broke my doggone leg, broke it off. So I went over to

---

* This hospital is near the Norfolk Naval Shipyard in Portsmouth, Virginia.
† The medical reports on Brashear's injury do not mention a Dr. O'Neill. His diagnostic summary from the hospital at Portsmouth, Virginia, does contain references to Captain G. J. Blacker, Medical Corps, U.S. Air Force.

the brace and limb shop and got me another one.

They said, "How'd you do it?"

I said, "I was shadow boxing." [Laughter]

People thought I was crazy, Stillwell. They said, "The fool doesn't have good sense." I was out shadow boxing and broke my leg.

Q: Can't keep a good man down.

Master Chief Brashear: So they fixed me up another one, and they were telling me how long it would take to make a leg and all this stuff. So I got in good with them. I'd go over there and work. I mean, I'd do everything around the hospital. I didn't want anybody doing anything for me. So I started working in the brace and limb shop, helping them out. I'd go sweep the shop, just do things. They made me a leg. They got it finished in December.

About the third or second of December, they gave me a leg, and I made a statement to the doctor. "Doctor," I said, "once I get a leg, I'm going to give you back this crutch, and I'll never use it again. I'm going to walk back to the hospital."

"No way! No way you can do that! Impossible!"

The day they strapped that leg on me, Stillwell, I gave those crutches back to those people, and I don't have one today, never used one, don't have one in the house, and I walked back to the hospital.

Well, then I had to say, "Now, how am I going to get out of Philadelphia back down to Virginia to be around that diving school?" So I called to try to get a tango number.[*] They wouldn't give me one. So I said, "Well, I'm just going to let it all hang out." So I caught a bus, came down to Portsmouth, tried to turn in at the naval hospital; they ran me off. They wouldn't let me in. So they ran me back to Philadelphia. So I got up there, and I raised so much hell, they got me a tango number and got me out of there, sent me to the hospital over here in Portsmouth.

---

[*] The Navy uses tango numbers to authorize transportation.

Chief Warrant Officer Axtell was the officer in charge of the diving school.* I sneaked off from the hospital and went over and saw him. He knew me from salvage school, and I said, "Ax, I've got to dive. I've got to get some pictures. I've got to prove to the people that I'm going to be a diver."

He said, "You son of a bitch, if something happens to you, you'll ruin my career!"

I said, "I know that! I know that!"

He said, "My career goes right out the window if I let you dive and something happens to you."

I said, "I know that, Ax. I've got to dive."

So he said, "I'm going to take a chance."

So he took a chance, and I got me a photographer. I dove in a deep-sea rig, dove in a shallow-water rig, dove in scuba gear, and got these pictures. I went back to the hospital, and I was on report. The nurse put me on report, see.

Q: For being gone?

Master Chief Brashear: Yes, being over the hill. She put me on report, and then she talked to me. She tore it up. So I said to myself, "I wonder how she's going to tear up the next one, because I'm going to be gone again." [Laughter]

I had to get some more pictures. So I left, came back over to the diving school again, and saw Ax. I said, "Ax, I've got to get some more pictures."

He said, "Okay, go on out there and tell them to dress you up."

So I got the pictures, and then they held my medical board at the naval hospital. I had those pictures. So the nurse put me on report for not being at the hospital, and Admiral Yon said that I shouldn't be like that.† But he talked to me about returning to diving and everything.

I didn't appear at the physical evaluation board. That created another big thing. I wasn't there. I was in Washington, D.C. They never did get me to a physical evaluation

---

* Chief Ship Repair Technician Clair F. Axtell, Jr., USN.
† Rear Admiral Joseph L. Yon, MC, USN.

board. I was supposed to go to one board, and it took them about six or eight weeks to set up another board. I was thinking in my mind, "Well, I'm not going to that one either."

In the meantime, they were getting tired of me at the naval hospital, so they sent me to the naval station for medical hold. When they would get a physical evaluation board set up, then I'd go back over there to the board, and that was just as good as I wanted. But between the naval hospital and the naval station, I endorsed my own orders and put, "FFT to the second-class diving school."* And I reported in to the second-class diving school.

When I told Ax about it, he laid some choice words on me, but he accepted me. I was an E-8 then.† And then it was time for me to go back to the physical evaluation board. BuMed was calling the naval station to inform me when I was supposed to go to the physical evaluation board.‡ But they didn't have me on the 1080. So you know what the old 1080 used to be?

Q: That's a printout of personnel.

Master Chief Brashear: Yes, a printout. I wasn't on the 1080 over there. They didn't know where I was. Finally, somehow or other, they found out I was at the second-class diving school. This lieutenant commander called me and said, "Where are you?"

I said, "I'm on this phone talking to you right now."

He said, "How in the hell did you get to the diving school?"

I said, "Orders, sir."

And, boy, what a confusion that made. So they told me to report to the physical evaluation board. And then I was put on report again. By then they were really tired of messing with me. But I'd sent all those pictures to BuMed along with my medical board.

So they said, "Well, if he did that down there, he can do it up here." So they called me to Washington, D.C., and I had to spend a week at the deep-sea diving school diving with a captain and a commander. Quite a few people from BuMed came over and watched me.

---

* FFT--for further transfer.
† E-8 is the pay grade for senior chief petty officer.
‡ BuMed--Bureau of Medicine and Surgery in Washington, D.C.

They watched me dive for a week as an amputee and run around the building, do physical fitness every morning, lead the calisthenics. I said, "Pretty good, a captain watching a chief work." I'd just wise off at them, you know.

So at the end of that week, they called me over to BuMed, had me stand outside of a door there like a dummy, and they were all sitting around a table. Captain Jacks was policy control, and he told me, "Any time you want, you can mention my name. I'm policy control." He said, "Most of the people in your position want to get a medical disability, get out of the Navy, and do the least they can and draw as much pay as they can. And then you're asking for full duty. I don't know how to handle it." He said, "Suppose you would be diving and tear your leg off?"

I said, "Well, Captain, it wouldn't bleed."

He said, "Get out of here. Get out." He ran me off.

So finally they called me back in. I reported back to the diving school. Axtell had been relieved by this time by Chief Warrant Officer Duell.[*] Axtell left word that I was coming back. Duell was the most efficient, conscientious, dedicated man I've ever seen in the Navy. He was a perfectionist.

They wrote him a letter telling him what to do to me. They wanted him to evaluate me for one year, and at the end of that year for him to write his report back to BuMed. You know, that man dove me every day, every cotton-picking day. I did it every day--weekends and all. At the end of that year he wrote the most beautiful letter. Boy, that was something. I was returned to full duty and full diving--the first time in naval history for an amputee.

Q: That's quite an inspiring story, Master Chief.

Master Chief Brashear: That was an accomplishment. Sometimes I would come back from a run, and my artificial leg would have a puddle of blood from my stump. I wouldn't go to sick bay. In that year, if I had gone to sick bay, they would have written me up. I didn't go

---

[*] Chief Warrant Officer Raymond K. Duell, USN.

to sick bay. I'd go somewhere and hide and soak my leg in a bucket of hot water with salt in it--an old remedy. Then I'd get up the next morning and run. I was to lead the calisthenics every morning with the students. Duell would be there. I was a chief. All the other students were white hats.* They never did get a chief while I was there. But I could hear them say, "That old chief--he's going to kill us." He gets out there, he ain't got no quitting sense on those calisthenics. He does this. He does that." They didn't know I was an amputee.

It just happened, the first two weeks we had orientation and physics. The third week in second-class school you go to the swimming pool. When I went to the swimming pool, I came out with my other leg under my arm. Those kids down there almost had a heart attack. [Laughter] Here was the same guy that was leading them, that they were talking about, had only one leg and was swimming them to death. But that would build those kids up, make them mad. That was sure a good motivational period for those kids.

Q: I'm sure it was.

Master Chief Brashear: At the end of that year, I was restored to full diving on full duty. I went to the boat house for two years of shore duty as the naval air station division officer.

Q: Why don't we resume that the next time we get together?

Master Chief Brashear: Okay.

Q: Thank you very much.

---

* "White hat" is a slang term for an enlisted person below the rate of chief petty officer.

Carl M. Brashear #2 - 92

Interview Number 2 with Master Chief Boatswain's Mate Carl M. Brashear, U.S. Navy (Retired)

Place: U.S. Naval Station, Norfolk, Virginia

Date: Friday, 2 March 1990

Interviewer: Paul Stillwell

Q: Master Chief, it's a real pleasure to see you again so we can continue your story. At the end of our last session, you talked about being restored to full duty after rehabilitation and then reporting to the boat house at the Norfolk Naval Air Station. Could you pick up the story at that point, please.

Master Chief Brashear: Yes, I'll pick up from the boat house at Norfolk Naval Air Station, where I served two years. At the end of those two years, I attended saturation diving training at the Experimental Diving Unit in Washington, D.C.

Q: What incidents do you remember from the Norfolk period in the boat house?

Master Chief Brashear: While I was at the boat house, I was division officer and also in charge of the divers. The boat house had four divers, and our primary duties as divers were search and rescue and recovery of downed aircraft and whatever other underwater work that we might have to do.

Q: Were you the senior enlisted man in this boat house?

Master Chief Brashear: Yes, I was the senior enlisted man, senior enlisted diver, and filling an officer's billet as division officer. During the period I was there, we had the opportunity to pick up a crashed helicopter off of the high-rise bridge near the Chesapeake Bay Bridge-Tunnel. We also picked up a helicopter that crashed at the end of the runway, right off of the boat house, plus doing underwater work on boats, ships, and aircraft. We would be called upon from time to time to go and assist the civilian divers in doing underwater work on the ships that were in the Norfolk Naval Shipyard.

Q: What sort of work did that include on the ships?

Master Chief Brashear: That included plugging up sea suctions, main circulation valves, taking off and putting on prop guards for the screws.

Q: When would you plug up a sea suction?

Master Chief Brashear: You would plug up a sea suction in case they wanted to repair a valve inside the ship. You would plug up a sea suction by putting a damage control plug in it or putting a cofferdam over the main circulation pump, where they could work on a valve or what have you on the inside of the ship. That was the purpose of that.

I recall working on the Forrestal in the Norfolk Naval Shipyard, and I was in scuba gear.[*] I imagine the Forrestal draws about 40 feet of water, and I was swimming under the Forrestal looking for the main circ pump. I didn't have enough clearance to swim under the ship before I hit the mud. The ship was just that close to the bottom.

Q: Less than a foot.

Master Chief Brashear: Less than a foot. I ran into mud under the bottom of the big, old Forrestal. It was black, and I didn't know where I was. That was quite a hairy situation there, because that ship was sitting that close to the bottom and I was under it in scuba gear.

---

[*] The USS Forrestal (CVA-59) was a large-deck aircraft carrier with a full-load displacement of 78,000 tons and maximum draft of 35 feet, 5 inches. The ship was eventually decommissioned in September 1993.

Q: So what did you do then?

Master Chief Brashear: Well, I found my way back and had to come back to the surface. I had to wait until high tide came in to raise the ship so I could go back and do the work then. At low tide, we just weren't able to accomplish our mission. So those were some of the things we got involved with while I was at the boat house.

Q: Could you describe some of the work on those helicopters and recovering those? How did you do that?

Master Chief Brashear: Well, while I was there, we had to attend a school that they call "aircraft and helicopter salvage methods." If a helicopter or a plane wasn't damaged severely, you'd go down and find the lifting points and place slings on it, lifting slings. We used the YD, which is a yard derrick that has a crane on it. We would make a moor and use the crane to pick up the helicopter or the plane.

Q: What precautions did you take to prevent further damage?

Master Chief Brashear: Well, I can't sit here and say what methods we used, because every salvage operation is different. You just have to use your own salvage experience and your own ingenuity and salvage this aircraft or helicopter without damaging it further. So you really don't know until you get on a job and actually start working. The first thing you do is make a complete survey of how the wreckage is on the bottom and just what you encounter.

Q: I imagine its position would be important, whether it was upside down or on the side or just what.

Master Chief Brashear: This plays a very important part--how she's resting on the bottom or what have you. You always try to bring it up as much intact as possible, where the people can investigate and make a determination of what caused the crash or what have you.

Q: How many men did you have working for you in that job?

Master Chief Brashear: As I said, we had four divers, but the total crew at the boat house ranged between 48 to 52 with three civilians. We had 14 boats. That included a diving boat, which was an LCM, landing craft mechanized, and that was equipped with scuba diving equipment, which is a self-contained underwater breathing apparatus, shallow-water diving equipment--you can dive to 130 feet--and, of course, the Mark V deep air equipment. When we had to use a crane, we would get it from public works. Or we even used a crane one time from the Norfolk Naval Shipyard to pick up a helicopter, because we didn't have one at the boat house.

Q: Handling that many men was a pretty good-sized administrative workload.

Master Chief Brashear: Yes, it was. It was a challenging job. I was the division officer. I had a lot of paperwork and a lot of administrative work. Plus, you had your civilians there with PDs, position descriptions. Of course, you got into a different situation when you were evaluating civilians rather than military people. So it was a good job, challenging job, and a lot of responsibility for an enlisted man.

Q: Did you contemplate becoming either a warrant officer or an LDO?[*]

Master Chief Brashear: Well, I thought about it from time to time. But, see, my primary goal was to make master diver, and if you accept a commission, then you cannot be a master diver. The requirement to be a master diver is E-7, E-8 or an E-9.[†] If you become

---

[*] LDO--limited duty officer.
[†] These are the Navy's top three enlisted pay grades: E-7, chief petty officer; E-8, senior chief petty officer; E-9, master chief petty officer.

an officer, then you can only be a diving officer, and also you can't have the responsibility of being a master. My primary goal was to be the first black master.

Q: Well, you worked so hard for it, you didn't want to get promoted out of it.

Master Chief Brashear: That's for sure. I didn't want to take a promotion. So what happened, Stillwell, after I made master, I thought about going from E-9 to W-3, but I was a little too old. And then I enjoyed being a master chief. There's an old saying in the Navy, you know: "The master chief knows everything. Then when you go to the wardroom being junior, you don't know anything."

Q: There's something to that.

Master Chief Brashear: So I remained an enlisted.

Q: How much training did you do in that job?

Master Chief Brashear: Well, what do you mean training?

Q: Well, you've got to train boat crews, you've got to train divers, and you've got to emphasize safety.

Master Chief Brashear: Oh, it was a tremendous amount of training. We would get at least four or five drills in a week just on rescue. We would simulate a crash and monitor how long it would take to get a full crew on our crash boat. It was a 63-foot crash boat that was equipped with gasoline Hall-Scott engines. From the time we'd sound the warning, we would try to get that boat out of the slip in 30 seconds. It was the ready crash boat at all times.

There was a tremendous amount of training there. Plus, there was a lot of training on showing films and slides and talking aircraft salvage. Or if an individual set his plane down, and he still had a few minutes to breathe on his oxygen, how you go about getting him out of there and not getting involved with the ejection seat. We had to train on the ejection seat, because if you dive on an aircraft, you have to know what not to touch getting a pilot out of it and not hit the ejection lever, because it will blow you away too. So it was a tremendous amount of training.

Q: You had to cover all the aircraft, presumably, that would land there.

Master Chief Brashear: Oh, yes. We had to know the lifting points and the ejection seats and different areas you can get yourself involved in in aircraft salvage.

Q: Did you have any actual crashes during that time?

Master Chief Brashear: Yes, we had an actual crash. One of the jets crashed over near Newport News. The pilot ejected, and all we had to salvage was the aircraft.

Q: Did you get any first-aid training in the course of that too?

Master Chief Brashear: Yes. You'd get your regular first-aid training, and we went through all types of artificial respiration when we started diving. It was arm-lift, back-pressure method, and then you've got the mouth-to-mouth resuscitation. It was quite extensive in medical and first aid.

Q: This was a far cry from the segregated Navy you had come into. Did you have any problem with people working for you who were uncomfortable with a black division officer?

Master Chief Brashear: Not at the boat house, I didn't. They were all very comfortable at this point.

Q: And you were the boss, so they had to do what you told them.

Master Chief Brashear: Yes, everyone was very comfortable, and I recall my department head gave me a letter of commendation for the improvements and for the morale and just the overall appearance of the boats and the boat house itself. I got a letter of commendation for the outstanding job I'd done while I was there at the boat house.

Q: Going back to your days in the presidential yachts, you knew what high standards were so you maintained them obviously.

Master Chief Brashear: Yes. I tried to maintain the high standards, and I think that's part of my nature. I've always had that "can-do" spirit, and so I think that stuck with me even until today. I think that's been with me.

Q: Well, just from what you've told me about your career, I imagine that the men working for you saw how hard you worked at it, and that would win their respect for you.

Master Chief Brashear: That was part of it too. I had some good people that worked for me there, especially two first-class boatswain's mates that I had. They were very outstanding. And then I got a chief machinist's mate, Chief Williams, who was one of my divers. We just had an outstanding team. I used the words, "We all played in the same court." So it turned out quite well.

Q: Anything else that you'd like to put on the record about that tour of duty?

Master Chief Brashear: Well, I would like to talk about one of my first-class boatswain's mates. I gave him a letter of commendation while I was there. At the boat house, we had two old Quonset huts that had been condemned.* I put in a work request to get public works to tear the two Quonset huts down. Three months went by. The electrician would come down and look at the Quonset hut and write up a report. About three weeks later, a pipefitter would come down. He would write up a report. Three or four more weeks would go by, and someone else would come down and write up a report.

After all this had been going on for a while, this first class boatswain's mate named Trumble said to me, "Senior Chief, when you going to take a day off?"

We were sort of on a first-name basis actually, and I said, "I don't know, Bob."

So two or three days would go by, and he would ask, "Senior Chief, when you going to take a day off?"

I said, "I will take a day off, and I'll let you know."

One day I told him, I said, "Bob, I'm going to take off tomorrow."

He said, "Good!" Then, about 3:00 o'clock in the afternoon, he came in and asked me to sign a chit for him to check out a two-and-a-half-ton truck.

I said, "Bob, what are you going to do with a two-and-a-half-ton truck?"

He said, "Well, I have bought some paint. I'm going to go pick up the paint." Well, I knew he was lying.

But what happened, Bob Trumble had rigged it up with the boat house crew, civilians and all, to tear these Quonset huts down. They started at 8:00 in the morning. They disconnected the electricity, disconnected the water lines, the radiators, and they demolished those Quonset huts. By midnight that night, they were at the salvage yard over in Camp Allen. When I came in the next morning, they were gone.

Q: Now, why did he want you to be off when that happened?

Master Chief Brashear: Well, now the reason he wanted me to be off during this evolution is because I couldn't have let them do it. This was taking away from public works, which used civilians. See, that's how the public works department made their money. Also, it was

---

* A Quonset hut is a semi-cylindrical metal building that can be shipped to an advance base area and erected quickly.

dangerous for my people to be out there disconnecting electrical lines from the base, steam lines.

Q: You couldn't officially approve of it.

Master Chief Brashear: I couldn't officially approve of it. But, of course, with me gone . . .

Q: You had no control.

Master Chief Brashear: He took the responsibility and took the Quonset huts down. When the public works foreman came down, he didn't like it at all. [Laughter]

Q: But there wasn't anything he could do at that point.

Master Chief Brashear: Right. And the department head, who was a full commander, told me, "Next time those sand crabs come down, call me." But the bottom line, Petty Officer Trumble, first class boatswain's mate, tore down two large Quonset huts in one day. It took public works nine weeks, and they'd just come down and inspect and write out job orders. Tearing those Quonset huts down was quite an accomplishment. It was comical after it happened, and it was a job well done.

Q: And you were proud of those guys too.

Master Chief Brashear: Yes.

Q: Do you have any other examples? I enjoyed that one. [Laughter]

Master Chief Brashear: Well, we just got a lot of things done. They would just keep our boats in top-notch condition and just morale-building things. Some of them would have their little slogans painted on the side of the cabin, you know, let them know whose boat it belonged to and just things of this nature.

Q: That kind of pride is very important.

Master Chief Brashear: Yes, it is. It's good for morale, and it's good for the people. Another thing was that they air-conditioned the place and paneled it. During that time, only GS-11s and commanders would have a place paneled.* But they paneled their quarters and did it on their own time.

Q: I bet they were pretty good boat handlers too.

Master Chief Brashear: The best.

Q: They had a good man teaching them.

Master Chief Brashear: They were the best. Yes, they were.

Well, you know, that brings up another good story. When the USS John F. Kennedy was placed in service in 1968, my department head asked me if I could control the Blue Angels from the water.† I said, "Well, I don't know." So he came down to me, and we went through a procedure how this evolution was supposed to be done. We went out and trained for two weeks prior to the Blue Angels performing, and I was to have a control boat in the center, and for me it would be a boat one mile away on either side of me, and I was controlling. The Blue Angels would come in from the boats a mile away, and then they would get by my boat, and this is where they were do their maneuver. I controlled them for 45 minutes, taking sextant angles from off the beach to keep my boats in position, and I'd

---

* GS-11 is one of the grades in the Civil Service personnel structure.
† The aircraft carrier John F. Kennedy (CVA-67) was commissioned 7 September 1968 at Newport News Ship Building and Drydock.

let the lead pilot know that I was in position. I got one heck of a letter of commendation for controlling the Blue Angels.

I asked one of the Blue Angels, "Are you guys crazy?"

He said, "No, but you are, because you're a deep-sea diver." [Laughter]

But it was amazing how those guys would get to my boat, and they would do their maneuver. It looked like they were going to run into each other. Sometimes I think they would be lower than my antenna on the boat. I controlled them for 45 minutes. That's the first time that had ever been done.

Q: Did you have radio contact with them?

Master Chief Brashear: I had radio contact with the lead pilot. I forgot now the calls we used, but I would let him know that we were in position and ready for run two, run three, run four, and that's when they would come in from the boats a mile away, and then they would maneuver from each other at my boat.

Q: Well, anything else from that tour?

Master Chief Brashear: That's about as exciting things as happened from that tour of duty at the NAS boat house, Norfolk.

Q: Then you went from there up to Washington.

Master Chief Brashear: Yes, I went from the boat house to Washington, D.C., in 1970 and attended saturation diving school at the Experimental Diving Unit. Saturation diving is diving at deep depths and remaining long periods of time. A couple of purposes for this are to measure the reaction of the body and to see how a body would adapt to deep depths. We dove there at 600 and 1,000 feet. And I completed that saturation training there.

Carl M. Brashear #2 - 103

Q: Well, now, when you say that kind of depth, are you talking about simulation? I mean, there's not 600 feet of water at Washington, D.C.

Master Chief Brashear: Yes, it was simulated in an igloo and a recompression chamber. The igloos have about 12 foot of water in them, and then you can pressurize them to any depth you would like to seek. You would work in the water for eight hours, and then at night you'd come back into the recompression chamber and eat, sleep, watch movies, make telephone calls to your girlfriend or wife or what have you. We maintained two dives while I was there, one to 600 feet and one to 1,000 feet. I completed that phase of training, and then I phased right on into master diver's training.

Q: What kind of gear were you wearing at those simulated depths?

Master Chief Brashear: We would be wearing what we call a Titan II. It's a helium mask that fits right over your face, over your nose, and you strap it to your head. It's on an umbilical, where you could swim out in the simulated distance wherever you wanted to go to. We were breathing a helium-and-oxygen mix. I believe it was a 94% helium and 6% oxygen. The reason for that is to give you an artificial atmosphere to maintain the mental and physical control of yourself at that depth.

Q: Do you have anything else on your body--a wet suit or just swimming trunks?

Master Chief Brashear: See, you can do that just in swimming trunks, because you can make the temperature of the water whatever is comfortable for the subjects that are down there. We used a four-man team. But now if you were diving off someplace like San Clemente, California, at saturation you may have to use a wet suit.

Q: And it's not going to be that warm at 600 feet.

Master Chief Brashear: No, no.

Q: What kind of sensations do you remember from being under that kind of pressure?

Master Chief Brashear: Well, it slows you down tremendously. You will be thinking you are doing a job, but you haven't gotten to it yet. Or you will be telling someone up at the surface that, "I'm getting ready to hook up this down-haul cable." Or "I'm getting ready to ride my bicycle." But you wouldn't be doing it.

Q: Is it hard to move your arms and legs physically?

Master Chief Brashear: No. No, it's not hard.

Q: It's just a mental thing?

Master Chief Brashear: Just a mental thing. And a lot of times nitrogen narcosis will build up, even though you are breathing that mixture of gas. You'll still get a little buildup of nitrogen narcosis like you're drunk or dizzy. Those are some of the effects that you get after you get to the depth. Going to the depth you might get some joint pains, or you won't be able to equalize your ears or something like this. You have to stop and come back a few feet to be able to equalize and then start down again. And you have different descent rates going down, whatever the mixture is, but you're not supposed to exceed 65 foot a minute.

Q: Could that be cured if they had more oxygen in the mixture?

Master Chief Brashear: No, that wouldn't solve it. It's just because you get too much oxygen, then you'll get into oxygen toxicity or oxygen poison. That would be the proper ratio at that depth. And it affects individuals differently, whatever the individual's tolerance is. That's why we use four subjects or four candidates, and we monitor the actions of each one of them. Doctors are monitoring you all the time, see.

Q: So this was strictly experimental?

Master Chief Brashear: Yes.

Q: What kind of conclusions did the experiments come up with?

Master Chief Brashear: They came up after extensive training and saturation that we can put a man down to the continental shelf and get him back. See, that was one of the purposes of it, too, to see how you get an individual back from that depth, how you're going to decompress him up here to get him back here to 14.7. I guess I can say this without getting in trouble. We hurt a couple of people, too, with this type of training, because at the early stages of saturation training, we would decompress all the time. When am I saying all the time, once we'd start decompressing, we didn't stop. But we found out that an individual has to have sleep. So if you go to sleep and you are coming up, you may not be able to equalize your ears. You're in a deep sleep, and it'll mess up your head.

Well, we've got people that can't hear at all. So we found at different stages that we'd have to let them sleep and not travel. So we would sort of adjust that to the individual. Whoever gets sleepy goes to sleep. But we tried to make it from around 12:00 at night to 6:00 in the morning you sleep, and you stop and everybody's awake. That remains also true in a recompression chamber. If you're treating somebody, you never move the chamber with a patient asleep. You always wake him up. If he doesn't want to wake up, slap him, do anything to him. Make sure he's awake and alert before you start decreasing pressure.

Q: That's surprising. I wouldn't have thought of that at all. I guess that's why they did the experiments.

Master Chief Brashear: That's why at the Experimental Diving Unit we like to say that we are some of the guinea pigs. We learned a lot. From the time I started diving, Stillwell, until the time I finished my diving career, it was amazing how some of us survived. We just learned a lot, and we were lucky in some of the things that we would do that were putting our life in jeopardy.

Q: Sounds like some were and some weren't. From what you say, some guys suffered from that.

Master Chief Brashear: Yes. Some guys are suffering from it now. Some people are walking around now suffering from decompression sickness.

Q: How does that affect you?

Master Chief Brashear: Decompression sickness can affect you in various ways. We have people that suffered from decompression sickness who cannot control their urine, cannot control their bowels, they don't have the articulation of their limbs, their arms, their vision. This is what we found out in the later years. When a guy gets a serious case of decompression sickness, they call it a CNS problem, central nervous system, and it cannot repair itself.

Q: Have you had any effects like that?

Master Chief Brashear: No, I've never had any of those effects. I got treated a couple of times for decompression sickness, but I think one time it was because I got hit so much in a boxing ring, I think that I was swollen, and we thought it was decompression sickness. But I think it was just getting hit so much in a boxing ring. But I was treated. We treat all doubtful cases.

Q: How long did that whole process take, where they would simulate you down to 600 feet and then bring you back?

Master Chief Brashear: Well, it depends on how long you stayed on the bottom. When I say "on the bottom," it depends on how long you stayed at 600 feet. One particular 600-foot dive, we stayed six days at 600 feet. It took us three days to get back because you've got different levels and different speeds coming up. And, of course, you'd have to sleep at 11:00 or 12:00 o'clock at night until 6:00 o'clock in the morning. So we had three days of decompression, and it was a total of nine days.

Q: How did you eat?

Master Chief Brashear: Well, I'll tell you. We'd work in the water for six or eight hours. Then we would exit out of the water back into the dry decompression chamber maintaining the depth. The decompression chamber has three locks. It has an outer lock, inner lock, and a medical lock that you can pass food through. Or you can pressurize the outer lock and take it down and equalize the pressure and send the food down. They've got a place in there where you can go to the bathroom, telephone, show the movie. All this is in the decompression chamber. The food doesn't taste too good. [Laughter] You can put all the salt on it you want, but you can't taste it eating in that helium atmosphere.

Q: You're just keeping your body going.

Master Chief Brashear: Just keeping your body going. But it doesn't have any taste to it. But that's how you eat and sleep in the dry decompression chamber. As I say, you can equalize the locks to take it down to whatever depth, then you can open the door.

Q: But all the time you're down there, your system is still like it's at 600 feet?

Master Chief Brashear: Yes. You are saturated to 600 feet. It takes a body about 12 hours after you reach a depth to become saturated.

Q: I've heard people who talked after they've breathed helium. Does your voice sound funny in that situation?

Master Chief Brashear: Yes. Helium contracts your vocal chords, and you talk like Donald Duck. Since I've been out of diving, I imagine they have methods now where they will unscramble that sort of method, and you almost sound your normal self. But you'll never sound your normal self. Even diving deep air you will get a different voice. It's amazing when you stay down to that depth and you step out of the chamber into this atmosphere we have here on the surface. Sometimes you'll stagger around, and you even vomit because it's just that shock to you.

Q: Regular life is so different from what you've been in.

Master Chief Brashear: Yes, you're just in a different environment, an environment that wasn't designed for a human being. And, Stillwell, it takes a special individual to be a deep-sea diver and to cope with different methods and different situations you put yourself into. I think that's one of the reasons our diving community never is--I guess right now we have about 5,000, including deep-sea divers, UDT, SEALs and all.[*]

Q: Did you go just to 600, or did you go all the way to 1,000?

Master Chief Brashear: No, just to 600.

Q: What were the effects observed for the people who did go to 1,000 feet?

Master Chief Brashear: It's decompression coming back, and, of course, you get more joint pains going there. That was about the only difference. And the breathing mixture, I believe, was different. The percentage of helium and oxygen, I believe, was different at

---

[*] UDT--underwater demolition team; SEALs--sea-air-land commandos.

1,000 than it was 600. I know 600 is a 94-6, and I believe it was a little less than 6% oxygen at 1,000 feet. Because, see, the deeper you go, you take that much atmosphere down with you, if you follow what I'm saying. On the 600-footer, we took a half an atmosphere down with us. What we try to say here is we pressurized a half an atmosphere on air. That stays with you all the time. It gets a little complicated. But we pressurized 16 or 18 feet on pure air. From then on down, then we pressurized on helium and oxygen. So you maintained that portion of atmosphere with you all the time.

Q: How has this been used in real life? Have people gone to those depths really, or is this all simulation?

Master Chief Brashear: People have actually worked at these depths, and I'm not that familiar now with what sort of vehicles we used at this depth. But the Mark I deep-dive system made a 1,000-foot dive and did a job. Taylor Diving Corporation--this is a civilian diving corporation--actually did a job or jobs at these depths. They have a pressurized vehicle that they can set over certain projects and stay in this atmosphere to do a salvage job. So it has proved effective and cost-effective, you know.

Q: What's the greatest actual depth you've been to?

Master Chief Brashear: The greatest depth that I've been to in open sea was 380 feet. That was in a deep-sea suit.

Q: So you do need some protection against that pressure of the water when you're out in it, I guess.

Master Chief Brashear: Yes, you do, and it depends on where you are as how much underwear you wear under your suit. Because, see, once you breathe helium, it's cooler anyway. It's cold, actually. So you need a lot of clothing on if you're diving like up in Iceland or somewhere up in that area.

Q: Any other findings from that time at the Experimental Diving Unit? Was that the project you were involved in?

Master Chief Brashear: Yes. That was the project that I was involved in. I trained there for six weeks and graduated as a saturated first-class diver.

Well, the commanding officer of the Experimental Diving Unit and the commanding officer of the deep-sea diving school said, "It's no need of sending him back. Ask him for a resume or a writeup, and we can keep him here for master school, if he's qualified." So I had a two-week period then from the time I graduated from saturation school until I went to master school if it was approved. So I wrote my paper to attend master diver school, and everybody approved it except about three masters. Three master divers gave me thumbs-down because I was an amputee. But they were overruled by the rest of the staff, and so I started master diver school in 1970.

Q: You use this term "master diver." What does that mean?

Master Chief Brashear: Master diver is a man that's proficient in all phases of diving. The highest position that you could hold in the diving community is master.

Q: What do you have to do to get that?

Master Chief Brashear: The first prerequisite to being a master diver is that you've got to be an E-7, E-8 or E-9. You have to have a well-rounded background in diving, and then you request to be evaluated to be a master. Then you go to the school, which is now in Panama City, Florida. You go before a board, and the board will talk to you while you are there, what got you there, what's expected out of you there, and what they intend to do with you. There is no flunking or failing or passing or anything of that nature in a master diver's evaluation. You make it or you don't.

So you will start five weeks of evaluation with four people watching you every day in all of the drills you can run. The people that are evaluating you are officers that are ex-master divers or master divers or the CO or the XO. They'll watch you every day, evaluating you. And at the end of that five weeks, either you make master or you don't.

Q: When did you make it?

Master Chief Brashear: June of 1970.

Q: And that was your goal all the way till then.

Master Chief Brashear: To be the first black master diver in the Navy--that was my goal. Well, back when they evaluating you there, they put a lot of emphasis on emergency procedures: what you do if you hurt somebody, how you treat somebody. That's treating for the bends, air embolism, pneumothorax, spontaneous pneumothorax. All the diving diseases and accidents that you can encounter, that's what they will evaluate you on, because those things can happen. Stillwell, you could make 4.0 marks on all of your exams and blow a drill or emergency and you would not make master.

Q: Because you've got to be able to react under pressure.

Master Chief Brashear: Yes. And they will try to get to you any possible way they can. If they can rattle your cage any way, they will do it, because this is what can happen out in the real world. If you don't have it there, you won't make master.

Q: It sounds as if you have a temperament that was well-suited for this, that you were calm and professional about the whole process.

Master Chief Brashear: There again, I didn't go out at night, I didn't have a beer. I wanted to be sharp. Every time those four pair of eyes said something to me, I wanted to be ready.

One time they came at me from all angles. It's a way to handle this. They were going to get to me, and I don't believe they would have really held it against me, but the commanding officer was yelling at me. They'd come at me from every angle, and I just told them, "Go away. I've got to do something to my diver." [Laughter] I thought I handled that one just real well. I didn't even respond to what they were saying. I had to watch my diver.

Q: You were doing the tending job then, I take it.

Master Chief Brashear: No. No, I was running the show.

Q: Oh, I see.

Master Chief Brashear: No, you don't do any tending there at master's evaluation. You run the show. You're the man in charge. They would do a lot of things to you. Like you were bringing a diver up and you shift him to pure oxygen. Well, then they'll get a senior officer to be on the rack, and they want to see how loud you can get to him. You might say, "Stand by to shift to O_2." Now, I do believe they already had the answer and just wanted to see how I was going to handle this--an enlisted to an officer. They'd see how you handle those situations. A lot of times he won't answer you, or he won't acknowledge, but you've got to get him to do what you want him to do. If you blow that, you're not going to be a good master diver. So they've got a good evaluation period, that that can happen.

Q: I think self-confidence would be important in this also.

Master Chief Brashear: You've got to be confident in yourself. You've got to know what you're doing and believe you know what you're doing and act it. It means a lot.

Q: Did you have competition from anyone else in this quest to become the first black master diver?

Master Chief Brashear: Yes, a man named Davis almost caught me.* [Laughter] As a matter of fact, when I lost my leg, he said, "I got you now."

Q: Real sweet guy.

Master Chief Brashear: He said, "I got you now." He said, "You ain't going to get it now." But I made it. I lost my leg and came back up that ladder again and made it. I made it about a year and a half, two years before Davis did. He made it in '72.

Master Chief Brashear: There were some other things. At one point in the master diver school I went to the chief petty officers' club one night, and this master diver--I won't call his name--but he got a little bit of beer in him, and he proceeded to give me a hard time about being a master diver candidate as an amputee.

So I went back to the school the next day and asked the training officer if I could lead the chiefs in calisthenics. So he said, "Yes, if you feel like you want to lead the chiefs in calisthenics." My intent was to get that dude that gave me a hard time and just wear him out. [Laughter] So he said, "Okay." He said, "You go ahead and lead them in calisthenics." I just wanted to get all the chiefs--no white hats, just the chiefs.

So the next morning, before I got ready to give them calisthenics, they backtracked on it. They said, "No, you ain't going to make a clown out of my chiefs in front of the students." So I didn't get a chance to lead the chiefs in calisthenics. But that's what I was wanting to do.

Everybody that the board accepts for master diver school gets five weeks of evaluation. It's set up so that once you start school, there is no way you can drop out. What I'm trying to say, you'll attend the full five weeks, and at the end of the five weeks then you go back before that same board again. Then they'll vote you a master diver, or they will decline you

---

* Master Chief Boatswain's Mate John Davis, USN.

as being a master. Well, there were six people in my class. Four of us made master and two didn't.

Q: Is that a pretty typical percentage rate?

Master Chief Brashear: Yes. Five or six candidates is all they have at one period, because four people watch you each day, evaluating you. And those four people are master divers or officers that are ex-masters. The only person that can evaluate you that's not a master diver is the diving corpsman. Of course, the diving corpsman cannot be a master diver, but he can evaluate you on your medical procedures.

So they start with five or six candidates, and you go the full five weeks. I was the last one that they called in, and they sort of had to stagger it. The first guy went in, he made master. The second guy they called in, he didn't make it. The third guy called in, he made it. Fourth guy called in, he didn't make it. The fifth guy made it.

Q: So you figured they were just alternating?

Master Chief Brashear: So I'm last. So they called me in. They said, "Senior Chief Brashear, the master diver's course does not give marks. Either you make it or you don't." They went on and on and on about what I'd been doing and where I'd been and all.

I said, "Please don't talk to me, if you don't mind! Get to the point!" And they would talk and they would talk and they would talk, talk about my physical stamina, what kind of shape I was in.

Then the CO said, "Let me tell you something. If there was a mark that we'd give, you made the highest mark of any man that ever come through this school to be evaluated for master." He said, "You did not make a mistake." He said, "We vote you master."

I just have to tell it like it is. All the black chiefs that were in that area knew that I was at the school. They were just sweating it out--was I going to make master? Was I going to make master? Had about eight black chiefs standing outside the school, and they found out

I made master diver, they carried me to the club bodily. So I was the first black master diver in the Navy.

Q: You had really worked hard for that one.

Master Chief Brashear: Oh, Stillwell, I burned some midnight oil. In the master's evaluation course, you can sit in the classroom and make 4.0 on every exam that you take, and you could go down the river and dive deep--they call it "going down in the deep"--and blow one of those dives and it'd wipe you right out. See, they mess with you all the time. Those four pairs of eyes are just beaming on you all the time. And then they role play.

One day I had a diver soaking at the ten-foot stop. Now, this was the CO. He came down off of the ladder. He said, "Senior Chief, you've got to do this! You've got to do this! Look what happened to this!"

But I just turned and walked off. I said, "I've got something to do with my diver." And then when I got my thoughts squared away, I turned around and said, "Now, what did you want, Captain?"

He said, "That's okay." [Laughter]

Because, see, what they're trying to do is try to get you riled up, and if you get excited and make a mistake with that diver down there, the same thing can happen to you out in the fleet, and then you'll hurt your diver.

Q: What all did they evaluate you on during this period?

Master Chief Brashear: Well, a certain percentage counts in the classroom on what kind of marks you make on your exam, and especially they weigh heavy on diving medicine and diving physics. And then when you get down the river, those simulated dives, you could surface a diver unconscious, know what to do with him in the chamber. Or you could surface a diver and he'd walk up to you and say, "My shoulder's hurting." Then you will simulate treating him in a chamber.

The main thing is his point of relief. Where he got relieved plays a big part on what kind of tables you're going to bring him back on or how long you're going to keep him there. Or you could have a diver pass out on the bottom. How are you going to get an unconscious diver back to the surface? You've got to touch all those bases, all those step by step by step, how you're going to treat this person, what can happen to a man. Or he comes up and they get him out of the suit, and then he falls down--how you treat him.

Q: What kinds of things would make the difference between passing and failing?

Master Chief Brashear: Well, say you've got a diver coming up on helium where you start shifting him to pure oxygen. After you get him shifted to pure oxygen, how long you're going to vent him, what time frame you're going to vent him, what pressure you're going to keep on your rack to get enough oxygen down to him to circulate his suit. If he does have an accident, how effective you are in giving orders and getting him treated. If you blow some of those, that's a bad mark against you and could wipe you out.

Q: So are safety and medical type things the main determinants?

Master Chief Brashear: Safety and medicine and physics.

Q: What qualities does a master diver need that those at a lower level don't need?

Master Chief Brashear: A master diver is required to treat all types of diving accidents. He's required to be able to supervise and manage all types of diving, submarine rescue, salvage, all phases of diving, helium and oxygen, air, pure oxygen and scuba, all phases. One prerequisite for a master is that he's required to have served a certain amount of time on an ASR, which is a submarine rescue vessel, and a certain amount of time on a ARS, which is a salvage vessel. You can be a deep-sea diver for years and years and years on a tender. It does not qualify you to be a master. And your quarterly marks have to be at a certain level.*

Q: Does this carry a high level of esteem in the diving community?

Master Chief Brashear: Tremendous amount. Tremendous amount of esteem. We've never had 100 master divers in the Navy. When I retired, I believe we had 59.

Q: It's a very exclusive club.

Master Chief Brashear: Yes, it is. And once you become a master, Stillwell, the only person on a ship that can relieve you of your duties is the captain. Now, on a ship where you have four or five diving officers, one of those diving officers is appointed as your diving officer, but he cannot relieve you of your duties. The captain has to relieve you, and then he'll have to put it in writing.

You have a tremendous amount of responsibility, too, because the welfare and lives of all those divers are in your hands. You're supposed to have the expertise that you can look at a man, and know if there's something on his mind that would mean he's not supposed to dive. Or if he's not acting himself, you're supposed to question him and see if he's in a frame of mind to dive. In other words, they're just your children. You have to look out for them because they belong to you. When I was at the safety center, I have found on diving accidents that I've investigated that the guy shouldn't have been diving because of his last night's activities. But the master failed to think about them.

I used to take them home--I call it "taking them home"--with me. I would think about each one of my divers, his personality, how he responds to different situations, how he acts under pressure. See, you have to know all of this. I've known my divers so well that if I was in charge I couldn't dive the same guy on different jobs, because he wouldn't be that

---

* These are the periodic evaluations on an individual's overall performance as a petty officer, both in his military duties and the specialties of his rating.

adapted yet, he wouldn't be that experienced yet. So these are things that a master gets involved with.

Q: Are there any specific incidents that you remember from that training period and the testing period in Washington? Are there any particular dives that you recall?

Master Chief Brashear: Well, I made a mistake while I was there in saturation that I had to call the doctor. I changed the depth of the chamber about 45 seconds before I was supposed to, and that could be critical. I had to wake the doctor up sometime during the day when he was getting his nap and tell him what I had done.

As far as the master's evaluation course, I'd seen the two guys make mistakes that didn't make master, but I didn't make any mistakes.

Q: What kind of mistakes did they make?

Master Chief Brashear: Well, one guy had the divers at the ten-foot stop soaking on oxygen. And two or three of those people jumped on him and said, "Have the green divers go ahead and unshackle the stage."

Well, he just stepped over and said, "Green diver, unshackle the stage."

Oh, that was the biggest mistake that ever he made, because when you're breathing pure oxygen, you aren't supposed to even make a move. Because, see, if you start working, breathing pure oxygen, then that will get your system where you can go into oxygen poison. Do you know what I mean? When you're breathing pure oxygen, you don't do a thing; you just sit there.

Q: So you've got to be clearheaded and know when to disobey an order.

Master Chief Brashear: Oh, yes. That's what it amounts to, or not listen to the captain or the exec. See, you just don't listen to them. But they've got this planned. Because if you're the commanding officer and I've got a diver here, you come down, you don't know what I'm doing. I'll tell you, "I can't do that." Now, if I was a captain and go down and say something to a diver or a diving master, I don't know. See, he'd have to tell me.

Well, if you're not thinking all the time, somebody will go to ask you to do something and you'll do it, and then it's wrong.

Q: So they were deliberately putting in traps to see how you would react.

Master Chief Brashear: Yes, to the real situation that could happen out in the fleet. So what happened here, the guy that unshackled the stage from the descent line, and the diver was on pure oxygen.

Q: So that was the end of him.

Master Chief Brashear: That's what caused him not to make master. And the other guy, I think his biggest problem--he had a casualty, and the point of relief in the chamber was 66 feet, and then he went on and took him to 165 feet. See, as I told you a minute ago, the point of relief has a lot to do with what depth you take. See, if you get relieved less than 66 feet, then you've got a different table to bring him out on.

Q: If a guy doesn't pass that course, is there ever a second chance?

Master Chief Brashear: They can give you a second chance if it's not too big of a flunk, and they will put it in your record whatever they recommend for you to do, "Beef up on this and beef up on this and return in such and such a time frame." Or they could put in your record, "Not recommended to return." That's left up to the board.

Carl M. Brashear #2 -120

Q: Anything else about that period of time to discuss?

Master Chief Brashear: No, it was just a happy day, about the tenth of June of 1970, when I made master. That was one happy day.

Q: Where did you go from there?

Master Chief Brashear: From there I went aboard the USS Hunley down in Charleston, which was a tender for nuclear-powered submarines, and served one year.* That was an exciting year for me. I was the R-7 division officer, which consisted of the divers, sailmakers, and the riggers. That was my first experience diving on nuclear-powered submarines and just regular old submarines, fast attacks and the boomers. Quite an experience diving around the cottonmouth snakes and alligators and what have you.

I spent a lot of time in the tech library learning about the nuclear-powered submarines, because, as I say, that was my first experience. That was a good education hooking up--I guess they call it the TDU--what pumps the residue of the nuclear-power waste into the ship. We had to hook that up from time to time to pump it into our tanks. And we had to hydrostatically test it to make sure it wasn't leaking.

Plus, I had to go through radcon school to be able to be a radcon worker, a radioactive worker. I dove around the submarines so much during that time as a master. I dove a lot as master, Stillwell. I wasn't like a lot of the masters not to dive. I dove with each one of my divers. I had 17 of them. So I'd make it a point to dive with each one of them. And my film badge read too high, so they had to take me out of the water for a while, because I was getting too much radiation.

Q: Is there that much radiation just external to the submarine?

---

* The submarine tender Hunley (AS-31) was commissioned on 28 September 1961. She was 599 feet long, 83 feet in the beam, had a draft of 23 feet, 4 inches, and displaced 19,000 tons fully loaded. She had a top speed of 18 knots and was armed with two 5-inch guns. She was built to service nuclear-powered submarines but was not nuclear powered herself.

Master Chief Brashear: Yes, it is, especially when you're hooking up the TDU. And it has a tendency to leak during the hydrostatic test, so you have to be down there watching it or feeling around it. And then you have to dive on the nuclear-powered submarines when the reactors are shut down. You have to dive on them when the reactors are critical. And then, I don't know how they expect you to do this, but they've got 20 foot, 10 foot and then you're diving in black water, and you're supposed to be able to know when you're within 10 foot of the reactor. [Laughter] So, anyway, those are some of the things that you run into there.

Q: So that means they're putting out radiation into water.

Master Chief Brashear: Yes. Yes, they are.

Q: I can see the value of you going down with your divers so that you can build their confidence, let them know what you're capable of.

Master Chief Brashear: Yes, and I just made it a point to dive with each one of them and let them know that I wasn't just only a topside master.

Q: Well, and also that's the way that you can evaluate how well they do.

Master Chief Brashear: Right. Yes. And there's a tremendous amount of diving on submarines. When a submarine comes in to the tender, you have to dive and make a security check. And then every other day you have to dive and make an underwater security check. Then you've got your ballast tanks you have to go inside and work on. You've got your missile doors. You've got your chain compressors.

Q: What sort of things were you looking for in these security checks?

Master Chief Brashear: Well, you were looking for foreign objects, somebody placing bombs or what have you, on these submarines, and just giving the underwater body a thorough check. Then you have that call at 3:00 o'clock in the morning that somebody's placed a bomb, and then you have to come back in and swim at 2:00 or 3:00 o'clock in the morning and show there's no bomb on your submarine.

Q: How could you see it?

Master Chief Brashear: Feel. Just totally feeling and swimming and feeling and swimming. So I got to the place where I would put a hogging line under the submarine and then move it two or three feet, and then divers swim back and forth, back and forth, feeling all around the submarine.

Q: Were there fake bombs put on in some cases?

Master Chief Brashear: We never found any fake bombs. We'd just get the calls. We have up to a three-and-a-half or four-knot current in Cooper River in Charleston, and if you lose a diver there at 2:00 or 3:00 o'clock in the morning, you're in a heap of trouble. About 500 yards the dry dock sits off of the submarine tender. Well, we would get calls that a bomb was placed on the dry dock. The dry dock was sitting out there in the middle of the stream, and you had to put scuba divers in the water at 2:00 or 3:00 o'clock in the morning to swim that dry dock. Dangerous, dangerous situation! It made your old heart beat fast, but I never lost a diver.

Q: They made you earn that master diver pay.

Master Chief Brashear: Yes, they did. Yes, they did.

Q: How well did the divers fit into the overall ship's company of the Hunley?

Master Chief Brashear: They fit in quite well, but on each ship you go on, there's going to be a little bit of friction between the divers and the ship's company, because someone's going to be uncomfortable with the divers getting incentive pay. And you always have got to curtail that as best you possibly can.

Q: How do you try to counteract that feeling?

Master Chief Brashear: Well, the way I try to do it is let them know that the diver school is open for everybody, and all you have to do is work and request to go to it and become a deep-sea diver and try to talk to them in those ways. I wouldn't go to an individual and say, "Well, they're better than you and this because they worked." They were just divers.

Q: They'd been through the training.

Master Chief Brashear: They'd been through the training. And then I would tell them a lot of times. There was one guy I had to talk to about it, and I said, "The other day when you were ashore at 4:00, what did you see those divers down there doing?" I'd say, "Liberty call goes and they don't even hear it. We've got work to do." I'd tell them about the divers swimming out in the cold water at 2:00 or 3:00 o'clock in the morning. So, you know, that's the way I talked to them.

Q: What kind of a place was Charleston to live in during those years?

Master Chief Brashear: It was all right. They treated me nice. I enjoyed it down there. The only thing I didn't enjoy was being on a tender. But that's the only job they had for me at the time is to serve a year on the tender before I'd get back to my ARS.

Q: Why did you not enjoy being in a tender?

Master Chief Brashear: Well, diving on those submarines was just repetitive, and I wanted to get out and work on wrecks. That's the type of diver I was. I wanted to go to sea and make things happen instead of sitting at the pier. That's what I wanted to get on.

Q: Charleston was probably a lot better place to live around 1970, say, than if you had been there 10 or 20 years earlier.

Master Chief Brashear: Yes. I was there in the '60s, and we only had certain places to go. Yes.

We had one exciting job while I was at Charleston. A submarine had returned from deployment, and this first class thought his wife had been messing around on him. So he went to beat her up. As a matter of fact, he stabbed her. Then he went next door to get her girlfriend, and her husband was home, and he punched him in his nose. So, in the meantime, he went up in back of a housing area called MenRiv Housing. I guess they named that after Mendel Rivers.[*]

Q: Right.

Master Chief Brashear: And up there in back of that housing, we found his clothes, his shoes, everything was on the bank. So we determined from that with the security that he had drowned himself. You could see the cottonmouths swimming on the surface. Big snakes!

So the security officer asked me if I would dive to search for the body. And I said, "Yeah."

---

[*] L. Mendel Rivers (Democrat, South Carolina) served in the U.S. House of Representatives from 1940 until his death in 1970. He was chairman of the House Armed Services Committee from 1965 until his death and was credited with getting a great deal of military money funneled into his district in Charleston.

So my divers told me, "You ain't getting me to dive in that water!"

So I told the security officer, "Well, my divers said that they wouldn't dive, and I can't dive in there by myself." I said, "My divers refused, and I can't order them." That's one thing: diving is strictly volunteer. I can't order them to dive.

So we went back to the ship. About 2:00 o'clock in the afternoon, a man named Steve Larson knocked on the CPO quarters door. He said, "Senior Chief, "I'll go with you."

Q: Was he one of your men?

Master Chief Brashear: Yes. I said, "Are your sure?"

He said, "Yeah, I'll go with you." Now, this was in August in 1970, I guess.

So we dressed up in wet suits, gloves, and everything, and we started swimming in that water around those snakes--you could feel the snakes bumping against you--and we found that body. The only reason that body didn't come to the surface was because that he was hung up in the seaweed. Oh, man, he'd been in the water about three or four days. Hot! We found him buck naked, but there wasn't a snake bite on him.

I thought that it was a courageous thing that that young man Larson did when he came to me and said, "Yes, I'll dive with you."

Q: It's a gruesome job.

Master Chief Brashear: Yes.

Q: Was there any difference in diving on an attack submarine instead of a missile submarine?

Master Chief Brashear: There's not that much difference. The old boomer is a bigger submarine, but the salvage inspection is about the same. They have what they call the chain compressor. We call it the anchor windlass, but they call it a chain compressor. It's aft on an SSN, a fast attack, and it's forward on a boomer. I guess changing a screw on a fast attack is a difficult job, because, see, the screw is forward of the rudder.

Q: So the rudder is in your way.

Master Chief Brashear: The rudder is in the way.

Q: Did you ever do that?

Master Chief Brashear: Yes, I changed one screw on a fast attack, and that's a big screw, 17,000 or 18,000 pounds. A lot of work. A lot of work.

Q: How is it attached to the submarine, bolts or what? And how do you take it loose?

Master Chief Brashear: Okay. Well, what you do, you will put the shaft on top-dead center, and it's got a padeye on top of the screw. That's the first thing you do is to put your padeye there to lift it. Then, see, you can't use any explosives on a submarine to blow it off the taper. So you back off on your spleen nut. You've got a big spleen nut right after you take off what you call your dunce cap. You take that spleen nut off of there. Then you've got a hydraulic system. That's sort of a complicated rig. You have to jack that screw off your taper. Then you have your crane hooked to it, and once you get it off the taper, then she comes out and you lift it out. It's quite a complicated rig.

Q: Sounds like it.

Master Chief Brashear: Getting all that hydraulic equipment set up on that shaft and the screw just exactly right. And on the inside of the fast attack, if you had to work on your seals from your shaft, you don't have as much of a compartment to put your inside seals on a fast attack as you do a boomer. And then you have to tag everything out on a fast attack.

And you've got a coupling--once you put your shaft seal on, if somebody goes down and cycles the rudder by mistake, then you'll tear that shaft seal off, and then you'll flood your submarine. But basically they're all the same.

Q: What other experiences do you remember from that tour of duty?

Master Chief Brashear: Well, that's about it. I was there only a year, and it was just quite an experience in learning the ins and outs of a nuclear-powered submarine. It was a good education.

Q: Then did you get an assignment of the kind you really wanted?

Master Chief Brashear: Yes. In 1971, I reported aboard the USS Recovery, ARS-43.[*] That was my home for the next four years.

Q: That's a long tour of duty.

Master Chief Brashear: Yes, and that was a good tour of duty. I was the master diver aboard there. We completed some good diving jobs on there and some good salvage jobs.

Q: Please tell me about them.

Master Chief Brashear: Okay. During that time, I had the opportunity to dive on one of the old coal-burning ships that was sunk out in the bay right off of Newport News. We dove on that and surveyed that. But we never did salvage it. We just went out to survey it. I think she sank about in 1918, somewhere along there.

---

[*] The salvage ship Recovery (ARS-43) was commissioned 15 May 1946. She was 214 feet long, 44 feet in the beam, had a draft of 15 feet, and a displacement of 1,995 tons. Her top speed was 11 knots.

Q: What was the purpose of surveying it at that late date?

Master Chief Brashear: Well, surveying it to determine if it was feasible to salvage it. But we found that it had too many holes in it, and it wouldn't be cost-effective to salvage it. We got a good picture of how she was lying on the bottom and almost determined why she turned upside down. See, she went bottoms up.

Q: Do you remember the name of the ship?

Master Chief Brashear: It was the <u>Monarch</u>.

Q: What might have been the purpose of salvaging such a ship, just to recover the metal?

Master Chief Brashear: Recover the metal and some training. See, this is good training for the divers. I think that would be the main purpose of it, and then, say, that we cleared the harbor in the case that we had to deepen the harbor.

Q: How deep was she?

Master Chief Brashear: Forty-four feet, I believe she is. So this was one of the jobs I did when I first went there. Plus, when we deployed to the Med, we'd be the standby salvage ship. I think I made three trips to the Med on it. Over there you had the opportunity to dive on merchant ships that had lost anchors and ships that steamed back from somewhere were hitting a growler or had a little hole in the side or something. So you'd have to do some underwater welding, underwater burning, this type of thing on board the <u>Recovery</u>.

Also, we went down off of Florida, I guess it was off of Jacksonville, to salvage one of the big helicopters. We lost a couple of tows that were very dangerous in getting them hooked up. You're getting involved in towing on those kinds of ships. And so I guess that was about the extent of that tour of duty.

Q: What kind of a atmosphere prevails in chiefs' quarters? I mean, you've got a whole space there full of experts in one thing or another.

Master Chief Brashear: Well, the atmosphere in my chiefs' quarters was great. We had good working relations. I more or less had control. And that was something I didn't work at; it just came naturally. I was the president of the chiefs' quarters and the chiefs' mess.

Q: How many chiefs were there?

Master Chief Brashear: We had eight. The exec didn't like to inspect the chiefs' quarters, which he was not required to do. But on the 10:00 o'clock inspection every morning, I'd like for the chiefs' quarters door to be open and let him look in and see how well we'd made up our bunks, because we'd have to go down and inspect our troops' bunks. That's one thing that I got the chiefs to doing. Everything had to be stowed, and everything had to have a place, and everything had to be in its place.

I recall in '74 I was in Suda Bay, Crete, Greece, working on a diving job about 3:00 o'clock in the morning. I got the word my father had passed away. I was picking up some anchor chain that one of the merchant ships had lost. So I flew back to the States and met the ship in Rota. Well, when I got back to the ship, they had a big sign on the chiefs' door. It said, "The Master Chief is returning! Stow your gear!" But in the chiefs' quarters, they must have gone to the lucky bag and had all of this junk thrown in.* [Laughter] Just had it thrown all over the chiefs' quarters, you know.

Q: They were yanking your chain a little bit.

---

* "Lucky bag" is a slang term for the space in a ship that serves as a lost-and-found area for unclaimed gear.

Master Chief Brashear: Right, right. So when you have that kind of an atmosphere, you know that the morale is pretty high.

Q: How well did the officers and the enlisted get together?

Master Chief Brashear: They got along great, very good, just got along beautiful.

Q: Did you have a special status with the CO because you were the master diver?

Master Chief Brashear: That, and I was master chief of the command. Well, I had an open-door policy to the exec or the captain. But I always performed my duty in a different manner from a lot of the master chiefs of commands. Periodically we'd have meetings of command master chiefs at the headquarters. Well, I would hear some things at those meetings that I didn't do, and I shared with them how I did my job. And some people are, in my estimate, just hard to listen.

When you're master chief of a command, if a young man wants to come and talk to you, it's a policy he doesn't have to go see his division officer or his leading PO or anybody.[*] He can come and talk to you. But if I thought it was something that the captain or the exec should know, then I'd go back to the division officer and tell him what I was going to do in case he wanted to defend himself. I just didn't run to the captain and exec and talk about somebody without first informing him.

Q: There may be another side to the story.

Master Chief Brashear: Right. Right. During the four years and eight months I was on the ship, with all the complaints I had, I only had two complaints during that whole tour of duty that had any validity for me to look into. There again, I went to the division officer. When

---

[*] PO--petty officer.

we looked at the situation, the division officer, said, "Damn, I made a mistake, didn't I?" And the chief said, "Man, we made some boo-boos, didn't we?"

And I'd like to share those with you. We had a black guy on the ship who was a second class. Well, when he would put in for a standby, the petty officers above him would put on his chit, "This man is not qualified to take care of duties," or "This man is not qualified." But here another second class would put in for a nonrated man to stand by for him, and they would approve it. So the second class came to me and told me about what was happening. I said, "Man, we've got to look into this!"

So I went and talked to the chief first. He said, "Doggone it, Master Chief, we made a boo-boo."

I said, "Yes, you did!" I said, "I've got to go talk to the division officer before I go up and talk to the exec, or even if I go to the exec."

So we went and talked to the division officer, and he said, "Damn, we made some boo-boos."

So we met--the chief, the division officer, and I--and discussed what could we do to please the second class. We wanted to handle it on our level and not take it to the exec and the captain. So I went to the second class and met with him, just the two of us, and I told him, "Well, they agreed that they made a boo-boo." I said, "What would it take to please you now to get this thing squashed? You're the man."

He said, "I don't know. I think the captain and the exec should know about it."

I said, "Okay. Think about it a couple of days." I said, "Now, this is what they will do. They'll call you and apologize to you. You know, that's a lot for somebody to come and apologize to you, especially one of those officers."

So he thought about it a couple of days and said, "Okay, Master Chief, let them come and apologize, and I'll forget about it." They did, and that was the end of that.

But of all the complaints I had, that was one of the few that had any validity to it. And he handled it in such an outstanding manner. You know, he didn't yell, he didn't curse, because he knew I didn't curse, anyway. And he brought that complaint to me, and that was really something to look into.

Q: What sorts of other complaints did you get?

Master Chief Brashear: We were in the Med one time, and we had some people that got in trouble. Now, this was a complaint. At the human relations committee meeting the whites brought a complaint that I would look after the blacks before I would look after the whites. And then I had to get myself in a corner and really look and see now, "How have I handled these things towards a black that I didn't handle them towards a white?" And I had to do some soul-searching.

Q: What did you come up with?

Master Chief Brashear: Well, what I came up with was that I had a tendency to talk to a black in a different way than I did the whites, and this was unconscious. If somebody hadn't brought it to my attention, I guess I would have kept on. So when they brought it to my attention, well, here again, I just apologized and said, "I'm sorry. I will try to correct it."

Q: What do you mean by a different way? More sympathetic?

Master Chief Brashear: A little more sympathetic in some areas, and especially when they extended this one guy on mess cooking. I went to the division officer and wanted to get him off of mess cooking. But, doggone, if you don't have a relief, you'll have to get extended. So I think that I had to correct myself in those areas.

Q: It's tough when it's an unconscious thing. As you say, somebody has to tell you what you're doing.

Master Chief Brashear: Yes. Yes. And I appreciated the man that brought it to my attention. You know, I went back and I said, "Thank you, partner. I appreciate that."

Q: Now, to what extent does the master chief serve as kind of a "sea daddy" for the junior sailors?

Master Chief Brashear: Well, he is the liaison between the enlisted and the chain of command. He's supposed to be there when they need him. If he can't solve the problem, he's supposed to be there to listen. Sometimes I found if you're just a good, effective listener and let somebody talk, they'll talk their problems out. That's the type of role that a master chief of a command plays.

No matter if it's with family or something on the ship, the master chief is supposed to be there. I've had the opportunity to talk to dependents, talk to wives. I had the opportunity to talk to one senior chief's daughter. I had to talk to him, a very serious problem. I had a senior chief on the ship that ran his daughter away from home because she was dating a black guy. He put her in the psycho ward. There were some serious problems.

So you get involved in a lot of things, being the master chief of the command. I had to do my homework before captain's mast, because the captain would look around and say, "Where is this young man from?"* You're supposed to know something about him, where he's from, basically what kind of background he had and everything.

Q: Well, that listening can be very important. If the sailor gets an idea that somebody cares, he feels a lot better.

Master Chief Brashear: Yes. And then I think I placed them in a comfortable position, too, because, see, I've never been a rowdy type of boatswain's mate and cursing and calling people bad names and saying derogatory remarks about sailors. I never did that.

---

* Captain's mast is a sort of court in which the commanding officer of a unit listens to requests, awards non-judicial punishment, or issues commendations. Most often captain's mast is used for punishment of lesser offenses than those that merit courts-martial.

Q: I've heard of boatswain's mates who do.

Master Chief Brashear: Oh. [Laughter] I'll tell you. Boatswain's mates, their middle name is "foul mouth." Seems like that went with them.

Q: That's part of the practical factors.

Master Chief Brashear: Yes. I'll tell you, I never practiced that. Thirty years of Navy, I never did that.

I lived on the ship a lot, and I recall one morning when the ship was getting under way. This young man had a car accident down in Smithfield, Virginia. He called the ship and asked one of his shipmates to come and get him. Well, the shipmate made all kinds of excuses why he couldn't go get that guy. Well, I called the exec. The exec came to the ship, took my duties, and I drove down and got him.

Q: You were the true shipmate.

Master Chief Brashear: Yep. Drove to Smithfield to get him.

Q: You've heard that saying, I'm sure, that a happy sailor is a complaining sailor. So you probably had to put up with some frivolous complaints, too, didn't you?

Master Chief Brashear: Oh, yes. You'll get those bitching sailors: "A happy sailor is a bitching sailor." That's what they say. [Laughter] Oh, yeah, I had to put up with all that. Yes.

Q: Kind of let that go in one ear and out the other?

Master Chief Brashear: Oh, yes. Yes. But we had one exec aboard the ship, and he called me up one time and asked me how did I get people to cooperate so effectively. I was the deck department chief also. We were towing targets out in Chesapeake Bay, and the seas were building up. I don't know if you know what a Williamson target is or not, but if the sea gets too rough, it will capsize one of those Williamson targets. So what you have to do is pick it up and put it on the ship.

Well, it was during mealtime, and my deck department wasn't large enough to handle this type evolution in rough seas. So I walked through the mess deck and said, "Sailors, I've got to get the target on board. I need your help." First class, second class, engineers, radiomen, ETs left their trays and came to the fantail, and we picked that target up.[*] The exec called me up and said, "How did you get those people to cooperate like that?"

Q: What was your secret?

Master Chief Brashear: Well, my secret is being fair as I possibly can. I like to say that I was a leader by example. I wasn't too proud to get out and lend a hand on any job we had at hand, whether it was diving or rigging or whatever, and I was always available when they needed me.

Q: When you've got some kind of a potentially hazardous evolution up on deck, how did you, in your own mind, avoid being overly cautious after what you had been through with your leg?

Master Chief Brashear: Well, I don't know. That's a hard question to answer. I don't know. But I haven't been overly cautious. You know, I'm always looking out for safety, but I don't go to an extreme because I lost my leg. I just look back at that and say, "Hey, it happened." And it was for a good cause, because none of my sailors got hurt. Each time

---

[*] ETs--electronics technicians.

you go on a salvage job in one of those ARSs, it's dangerous. But I don't go overboard with it.

The chaplain asked me that question, too, once when we were doing the movie. When I did the movie called "Come Back" he said, "How can you come back and live some of these scenes?" Well, I guess it's just my attitude.

Q: You focus on the job instead of on the problems.

Master Chief Brashear: Yes.

Q: Were the officers in that ship mustangs for the most part?

Master Chief Brashear: Most part were mustangs. When I went aboard the <u>Recovery</u>, our skipper was an ex-chief signalman. The exec was an ex-chief quartermaster, I guess. Then the boatswain and the engineer were ex-enlisted. And the first lieutenant, who was a jaygee, was ex-enlisted.* So on diving ships like that during those years most of the officers were mustangs, LDOs.

Q: I'm sure there was a lot of camaraderie and togetherness in the whole ship.

Master Chief Brashear: Yes. Like a big family, and it's not very hard to determine who's not carrying his weight, you know, because you've got a small ship. Captain Clark was the first skipper I had on an ARS. He was sort of a comical guy. And then the guy after him was named Bonham. He's a four-striper now. Now, he wasn't a mustang, but he was a youngster, and that crew would cooperate with him so well. He just had that act. He was fantastic.

Q: Was there anybody else that had near the diving expertise that you did?

---

* Jaygee--lieutenant (junior grade).

Master Chief Brashear: No, I had three chiefs that were divers, and none of the white hats had the experience that I had.

Q: So, really, you got to call all the shots on diving, I expect.

Master Chief Brashear: Well, yes and no. You don't know everything, and some of those guys brought a lot of experience to the ship from the different situations they had been in. So before I went on a diving job, I liked to have what I call a rap session. I'd always tell my divers, "I'm not perfect. If you see me make a mistake and you don't stop me, I'm going to punch you in the nose." [Laughter] You know, that was my attitude. I said, "Gee, we're all divers. We all go through these schools. Don't you let me make a mistake." I had a sign on my diving locker, "There's no one of us smarter than all of us." And I believe that.

Q: That's a good way to put it.

Master Chief Brashear: We would have a rap session how this job should be done or how we thought we were going to attack this job. Whether it was pulling a ship off the beach or for training or diving on the real thing, we'd talk about it. Then, when we went to the diving station, there wasn't a lot of talking or yelling. That's the way we agreed to do it, and that's the way we did it.

One of my chiefs was a second-class diver, and I couldn't get him to go to first-class school. He said he didn't want to dive on mixed gas. He said he wanted to stay a second-class diver. And then before that tour of duty was up, they disqualified all the chiefs that were second-class divers. If they refused to go to first-class school, they just took away the qualification.

Q: Anything you remember specifically from your Mediterranean deployments? Any incidents, either liberty or salvage jobs or what have you?

Master Chief Brashear: No, nothing that rings a bell, other than picking up those anchors that the ships had lost. I can't recall anything.

Q: Part of your job was just being available and ready in case something happened.

Master Chief Brashear: Yes. We'd get involved in some diving jobs that you don't know how you get involved in. I remember the USS Patterson. The Patterson had a variable-pitch screw on it, and so they couldn't get it out of the back pitch. We dove on that quite a bit to see what was wrong with it, couldn't find why they couldn't get it out. We ended up towing that ship from Suda Bay, Crete, back to Naples, Italy. And that was sort of exciting doing that.

Plus, we had to dive in the engine room on the Saratoga. It was the first carrier that went through the SLEP program.[*] But she flooded the engine room over there in the Med, and we dove on the engine room to see why it flooded.[†] So our skipper told the captain of the Saratoga he'd tow him back to Naples.[‡] He said, "No, you won't. I'm going to steam back." Proud captain, you know. So he steamed it back to Naples after flooding in the engine room.

Q: What do you remember specifically about that job?

Master Chief Brashear: Well, just the hazard of diving in the engine room.

Q: How did you get into it?

---

[*] SLEP--service life extension program.
[†] The accident on board the Saratoga (CVA-60) occurred in August 1971 at Piraeus, Greece.
[‡] Captain James R. Sanderson, USN, commanded the USS Saratoga (CVA-60) from 7 August 1971 to 16 February 1973.

Master Chief Brashear: Well, you go down to the hatch, and then if you have to bend the rules a little bit and dive in scuba, you have to have a tending line. So it's breaking the rules a little bit. We tried to determine why they flooded the engine room, but we never did, just didn't do it. So he steamed her back to Naples.

Q: I never heard about diving inside a ship before.

Master Chief Brashear: Oh, I've dove inside a lot of wrecks, but I'd be in a deep-sea diving suit.

Q: Well, I'm thinking of a ship that's operating.

Master Chief Brashear: Yes. It's a hairy situation when you get down in the engine room and you can't see a doggone thing.

Q: Well, from that ship you went to the safety center in Norfolk, where Admiral Dunn was the commander.* I wonder what you remember about him. He certainly remembered you when I told him I was going to interview you.

Master Chief Brashear: Yes, I worked for Admiral Dunn at the Naval Safety Center after I left the <u>Recovery</u>. He thought that it was sort of impressive--every time his master diver would go out, I'd come back and somebody would send a message, a bravo zulu.†

Q: That's the kind of thing that would get his attention.

Master Chief Brashear: Yes.

---

* Rear Admiral Robert F. Dunn, USN, served as commander of the Naval Safety Center from October 1976 to August 1977. The oral history of Dunn, who retired as a vice admiral, is in the Naval Institute collection.
† In the Navy's signal book, the phonetic alphabet letters bravo and zulu are used together to mean "well done."

Q: What kind of a guy did you find him to be?

Master Chief Brashear: Well, I just don't have the words to explain the type of guy he is. He's just an outstanding guy, outstanding to work for, concerned about the least minor detail. When I worked for him at the safety center, he was just a nice guy. You could go talk to him, and he would listen. If he had something to say, he could say it to you. And then if he wanted to shoot you down, he could say it to you and make you like it. He was just an all-around nice, nice guy.

Q: He's one of the friendliest admirals I've encountered.

Master Chief Brashear: Oh, my God, yes! He would walk through here after I was working here, and he'd stop and talk to me out there, you know, and just a great guy. I went to a prayer breakfast. I went to the chiefs' club one morning. He left the rest of the dignitaries and came over and talked to me, just from knowing me at the safety center.

One job I did at the safety center saved the government thousands and thousands of dollars. During my tour of duty there, we had the Mark I dive system, and people had had some accidents with it. So I headed up a tiger team and conducted a field change on the Mark I dive system band mask throughout Europe--that was civilians and all--and got a letter of commendation for that. I did a field change on the breathing mechanism, and I did a field change on the bail-out bottle connection. Then I bench-tested it, it proved satisfactory, and NavSea approved it.[*] Admiral Dunn thought that was the greatest thing that ever happened.

Q: What kinds of other jobs did you do at the safety center?

---

[*] NavSea--Naval Sea Systems Command.

Master Chief Brashear: My primary job there was to investigate diving accidents. I would do an analysis to determine what caused the accident and write recommendations how to prevent more accidents in the future.

Q: Turned you into a regular bureaucrat.

Master Chief Brashear: Yes. And I was required to conduct safety presentations--I've forgotten now how many I was supposed to do a year--at different diving activities, all when I was requested to come to give a safety brief.

Q: Did you work strictly in the diving area, or did you get into other things as well?

Master Chief Brashear: No, I was strictly a master diver for the United States Navy, and you couldn't get in any other areas having that job. I lived out of a suitcase. I was always on airplanes going to the Med, Europe, Pacific. I was all over the place in those two years I was there at the safety center. One year I investigated 86 accidents, and that's quite a job, plus, answer all the "safety grams" that you get and look into different situations, plus giving presentations.

Q: Could you take a couple of accidents, for example, and just describe what you went through during your investigations?

Master Chief Brashear: Yes. I can mention one when I went to Coronado. A young kid drowned, and he was in a self-contained breathing apparatus, semi-closed circuit. What I mean by semi-closed circuit is you only make bubbles to the air once your breathing bags overcome the bottom pressure. Then you make a few bubbles here and there. This is for sneak attacks. So what had happened, was that a group of SEALs had PT in the morning, and I've forgotten, but I think they had returned off of a five-mile run. Then this one man immediately got in his swim gear and went swimming. Well, oxygen built up, and he had oxygen poisoning. He most likely swallowed his tongue or else passed out and drowned.

But what happened is when he came off of that run, he hadn't calmed down enough. And when they put him in the breathing apparatus, he didn't purge his bags, and all of that oxygen built up, plus his oxygen, and he had oxygen poison and drowned. So we determined from that job that you've got to give a guy an ample amount of time to calm down and breathe normally and make sure the bags are purged good before you put him in the water and let him go swimming. So that was a human error.

Q: So many of those safety precautions come about from losing somebody.

Master Chief Brashear: All of them are written in blood. So that was one big mistake that I found. Plus, I investigated another accident that was in California also. It involved a lieutenant (j.g.) who wasn't experienced in scuba diving. Well, he was about 90 feet below the surface, and he started breathing hard. Well, when he started breathing hard, he thought his tanks were empty. So he went to his buddy to get some gas or get some air--we call it gas--but he was too far from his buddy to make it. So he started to the surface. Well, he held his breath too long, and he caused himself to have an air embolism. So when he got to the surface, he was passed out, and the people on the surface didn't treat him properly, and he had permanent damage.

Q: What are some of the other cases you remember?

Master Chief Brashear: Down here on the L. Y. Spear, one of the divers was diving 16 or 18 feet, and a Grove reducer carried away.* Now, this was a mechanical failure. A Grove reducer carried away and blew 2,000 pounds of air right in his lungs, and blew him up a little bit. Well, let me see. They called me at the safety center, and by the time they got a hold of me, they had contacted the police also. We left the safety center, and I drove out the gate at 60 miles an hour and went down to the Spear and treated him. He was asymptomatic when I got him back to the surface. That was one accident I looked into.

---

* The USS L. Y. Spear (AS-36) is a submarine tender.

Q: Did you do any diving yourself during this period?

Master Chief Brashear: I only made one dive during this period, and this was at the escape training tank in Hawaii. I went out there to dive and to reevaluate the Stenke hood. The Stenke hood was a buoyancy compensator, you might call it, or a life vest so that if you made a free ascent out of a submarine, you could breath normally all the way to the surface. I talked about Lieutenant Stenke earlier, from my time aboard the Coucal with him. So I went out there to evaluate that, and I think that was about the only time I was in the water other than at the safety center, while I was there, they made the short movie called "Come Back" with James Whitmore. I had to go swimming for the underwater photographers to take pictures of me to make that movie. I made my regular requalification dives--four every six months.

Q: How did the movie come about?

Master Chief Brashear: Well, while I was at the safety center I started getting a lot of TV coverage. I had been in various newspapers and magazines, and Bob Manning at Chinfo recommended that they would do a short movie of me to be a filler or something on TV.[*] So they made about a four-and-a-half minute movie of me for TV. From that, when the "Come Back" series started, Bob Manning recommended that I be one of the candidates they do for the program.

Of course, "Come Back" is a documentary that is made of people that had a downfall and made a comeback. That's how it got the name. That year they did myself, Neil Sadaka, Freddie Fender, Rosemary Clooney, and Bill Veeck. Each of us had a 30-minute documentary. So that's how that came about. I had to do some swimming and running so they could get footage while I was at the safety center.

---

[*] Chinfo--The office of the Navy's Chief of Information. Robert Manning worked there as a civilian.

Q: Did you miss not diving as much as you had before?

Master Chief Brashear: Yes, I did. I'd get sick when I'd go see somebody in the water and couldn't get there myself. I miss diving.

Q: I can't imagine that the paperwork was all that much fun, especially since you were dealing with unhappy reports.

Master Chief Brashear: Yes, there was a steady flow of paperwork. The first time I had my eyes examined for reading glasses was while I was at the Naval Safety Center. You sit there and read thousands and thousands of pages. You had to review all dives and pull out all the accidents. So I was reviewing the records of anywhere from 80,000 to 120,000 dives a year.

Q: You can't give each one very much attention at that rate.

Master Chief Brashear: Well, you get to the place where you'd look at the longitude, latitude and the code numbers, a couple of code numbers tell you whether it was an accident or a regular dive. A couple of them that I took a little patience with and looked at the longitude and latitude, and they were diving in the desert out in the West. [Laughter] But that didn't mean a lot, you know. You know, some guy would put down the wrong numbers.

Q: Did you put out periodic bulletins or "safety grams"?

Master Chief Brashear: I'd write "safety grams" and answer "safety grams" that required answering. I've forgotten now how many safety notes that I'd write a year pertaining to diving. I recall one safety note that I put out--that if you had a wet suit diving in tethered shallow-water equipment, you weren't required to wear a life jacket.

This lieutenant (j.g.) called me up, and he said, "Well, I don't think that's right. I think a diver should have a life jacket on."

I said, "Sir, that's a recommendation. If you want to wear two life jackets, put them on. I just recommended that it wasn't required. But it's your show!"

See, that's what I used to tell people, "It's your show! I'm just saying that it's not mandatory, but if you deem it necessary that your divers want to wear a life jacket, or you should happen to wear a life jacket, have them to wear it."

Q: I can think of a situation in which that would be harmful if it brought a diver up too quickly.

Master Chief Brashear: Yes. Yes. But here again, if you go inspect a diving facility, and he has a cartridge in his life jacket that's too big, then that's a discrepancy. Because, see, some divers will put in a cartridge that's too big to bring him to the surface. But that's not the purpose of a life jacket. A life jacket never was designed to bring you to the surface. A life jacket is required to keep you on the surface. See, if they bring you up too fast, then you're going to embolize. But a lot of those guys will cheat and put a bigger cartridge in there saying, "If something happens to me, I'll pull this rip cord, and I'm going to get lifted off the bottom." But you don't do that. It's designed to keep you on the surface. And if you get down on the bottom and get to working and that little string comes out of there and gets caught on something and pulls it, you could hurt yourself.

Q: What else do you recall about that job?

Master Chief Brashear: Well, that's about all I can remember about the Naval Safety Center.

Q: We haven't talked much about your domestic life. At what point did you get remarried?

Master Chief Brashear: I was single when I went to the safety center. While I was at the safety center, I would meet with the master chiefs like I did when I was a command master chief, and then we would take tours around different clubs. I went to the initiation down to the chiefs' club here on the naval station, and I met this lieutenant. So we fined her for being in the chiefs' club during initiation according to how many stripes she had, and she didn't want to pay. Well, since she didn't want to pay, we were going to put her in leg irons and handcuffs and arrest her. But we decided, well, we'd give her a break, and all we had to do to her then was put a white hat on the head of one of the new chiefs head and then hit it with her fist and break the eggs. So we finally got her to do that. So that's where I met my second wife.

Q: She was the lieutenant?

Master Chief Brashear: Yes. I met her while I was at the safety center, and we started dating. Then we got married, and my domestic life was pretty good up until I retired out of the Navy. After that I went to college, and I think I was around her too much. We didn't get along after that, and we got divorced after she made captain. She's still on active duty.

Q: What's her name?

Master Chief Brashear: Hattie Elam.[*] She went back to her maiden name after we got divorced. Right now she's the chief nurse and director of nursing at the naval hospital in Charleston, South Carolina.

I was married to my first wife for 21 years. She and I had four sons together. And alcohol fouled me up in that marriage. I got to be an alcoholic. Well, I'm still an alcoholic, just recovering. But I got to the place I'd drink too much and sort of fouled up my first marriage.

---

[*] Captain Hattie R. Elam, Nurse Corps, USN.

Q: Was there not some sort of prohibition against fraternization between officers and enlisted when you were dating the lieutenant?

Master Chief Brashear: Well, we didn't have that problem. She seemed to think that she did her job in the Navy, and what she did with her private life was her business. But some of my shipmates and some of my associates and friends said that, in their opinion, the reason we didn't have any trouble was because of my status. I'd been on TV. I did this, and I did this, and I'd been in magazines. But we would talk to people that just had a lot of trouble, enlisted and officers.

As a matter of fact, a lady used to come to our house, and she was a lieutenant dating a first class. She was having a lot of problems. But we never did. She got deep-selected for commander. Admiral Watkins thought it was funny, you know, a master chief taking care of a captain.* [Laughter] So we never had any trouble, none whatsoever.

Q: Until you had too much togetherness.

Master Chief Brashear: I think that was our problem. We had too much togetherness. We talk about it now. We visit, we date, actually.

Q: Where did you go from the safety center?

Master Chief Brashear: From the safety center, I went back and served two years on the <u>Recovery</u>, then retired.

Q: I would think that would be kind of a letdown, because you had already proved that you could do that job.

---

* Admiral James D. Watkins, USN, served as Chief of Naval Operations from 1982 to 1986.

Master Chief Brashear: Well, it wasn't really a letdown. I think it was a feather in my hat that they wanted me back aboard. The ship was the same, but the jobs were not the same. Every diving job, every salvage job is different. And I just think that it was a feather in my hat that I got to go back aboard ship.

Q: I know you enjoyed going back to diving.

Master Chief Brashear: Yes. So I went back aboard there, and I'd been there getting ready to retire, and I started drinking too much again. So I turned myself in at the naval hospital in '78 and went through the alcoholic rehab program. It was there that I made the decision to retire.

Q: I'd be interested in your talking about that program for the benefit of others. What ways did that help you?

Master Chief Brashear: Well, if you work your program effectively and do your inventory every day and do your psychodramas, as they call them, the psychiatrists and staff can almost determine why you drink. When you do your collage, the collage tells you a lot about yourself. I worked my program the best that I possibly could. I put all of my heart into working my program.

Q: That's the way you approach anything.

Master Chief Brashear: Yes. The collage involves fantasizing from as far back as you can remember up to the present point. In my collage I was a little boy, and the sun was coming up, and I had that adventurous spirit. You know, I just wanted to get out and have adventures. At points in there I would slip away from home and swim across creeks, lakes, ride motorcycles, do dangerous things, leading up to just everything being exciting.

Well, at one point in that collage I dated a young lady before I joined the Navy. I wanted to join the Navy and send her to nursing school. Well, her mother thought I wasn't educated enough, being a farm boy who hadn't finished high school. So she'd keep running me off, and I joined the Navy. While I was in the Navy, the young lady met a guy who was a captain in the Army, and they got married. Well, at the center of my collage, I had a big picture, two big eyes staring up; beside it was a little bitty picture of a nurse. Even when I was married to my first wife, see, I didn't treat her nice. All the women I dated were nurses.

Q: And then you married one.

Master Chief Brashear: Then I married one. So they almost determined from the way I worked my program and my inventory every day that I hadn't gotten over that young lady, and I kept trying to make my first wife into her. Exciting.

Q: That is interesting.

Master Chief Brashear: Interesting. And I would just tell everything that went on. As I say, I worked my program the best I could. When I did the psychodrama, I wanted to do one with my father. They thought my father didn't give me enough love. I thought that because he never put his arms around me. People didn't do that in those days. We did a psychodrama, and a guy played my father. That didn't show anything. A guy played my first wife. That didn't show why I drank. But, you know, when somebody played Anna Jean--that was the young lady's name--you know, it was a lot different. My emotions were different. So maybe that's part of my problems.

Q: Were they able to cure you?

Master Chief Brashear: No. No, they weren't able to cure me. They weren't able to write in my record at the end of my six weeks that I was going to recover. They wrote in there, "It's a doubtful case that he will recover."

Q: Well, have you since put the kind of effort into that that you've put into everything else?

Master Chief Brashear: Sure, I'm sober as a judge. They were wrong. I haven't had an alcohol-related speeding ticket or incident since 1978. I can't say I haven't had a drink. But I can from this day forward, I may not ever have another one, but I've had a drink since '78.

Q: How did you succeed when they predicted that you wouldn't?

Master Chief Brashear: Well, I proceeded to not lead the life that I had led before where booze was concerned. I developed an attitude that maybe they could be wrong, which they were to a certain extent.

Q: Did the discovery about this nurse help you deal with it?

Master Chief Brashear: Yes, it did. Yes, it did. Stillwell, I learned so much about myself during those six weeks, it was pathetic. I'd sit at 12:00 o'clock at night writing an inventory to give to my counselor for them to study. I learned a lot about myself.

Q: Well, at least if you know what the problem is, that can help you solve it.

Master Chief Brashear: Yes. Yes, it can. Yes, it can. Deep down inside, there was a lot of emphasis placed on that nurse and that lady because my collage had those big eyes just like she's saying, "You get away from me!"

Q: You never know how your life would have turned out if her parents had had a different attitude.

Master Chief Brashear: Well, when I go back home now, I hear some things that her mother has said about me. She said that she wished she hadn't interfered because her daughter's been divorced and married again, divorced and married again, and not getting along well now. So I've heard that from different people. I went to visit her mother a couple of times when I was back there. She just looked at me and sort of smiled and said, "You've done wonderful."

The guy that married her, he carried her to D.C., and he beat up on her a lot. Finally she couldn't take it anymore, and she came back to Kentucky and married someone else, and they got divorced. She married this guy now. She's been married quite a while. But I understand that there's nothing exciting about it. I think he drives a Cadillac and won't let her drive it. [Laughter] So that's the way that went.

Q: Well, you've got to live the life you have instead of the one that might have been.

Master Chief Brashear: Oh, yes.

Q: What sorts of withdrawal symptoms did you have getting out of the Navy? This had been your life for 30 years.

Master Chief Brashear: Well, when it came time to get out of the Navy, I'd wake up some mornings and I would be so afraid, butterflies in my stomach, just afraid. What am I going to do when I get out? What kind of job am I going to get? Just mixed emotions. It was frightening, knowing that I grew up in the Navy from the time I was 17 years old. Now I was 49 years old and had to face that outside world.

Q: Did the fact that you were a celebrity help face this new world?

Master Chief Brashear: I don't think that helped at all, and I don't know about being a celebrity. I'd just been exposed to a lot of TV coverage and magazines.

Q: Well, most of us haven't had that kind of coverage.

Master Chief Brashear: Yes. But I was afraid. I retired on the first of April, 1979. And what a retirement, Stillwell! What a retirement! I was going to retire aboard the <u>Hoist</u>. That's the ship I lost my leg on. But it got too big, so they had to move it to the gymnasium at the Little Creek Amphibious Base. They had it on the news about three days prior to my retirement, had posted all over the amphibious base that I was retiring. They had a big banner across the gate. They had two TV stations there. Just a gymnasium full of people.

Q: That had to make you feel good.

Master Chief Brashear: Yes, yes. So we had a few admirals there and generals and captains. The gym was full. They opened up the gates. That was quite a day. So I retired, and they had the reception at the Wheel House; people were outside lined up.

We were living on Hialeah Street in Virginia Beach. So I went to QED one day to see Norm Chalmers.[*] He was a captain I used to work for. He was the vice president of QED.[†] So I just went over to see him. I had no mind of going to work. I just went over to see Norm Chalmers.

Norm said, "I've got a job for you."

I said, "No, you don't." I'd only been out of the Navy 19 days.

He said, "I've got a job for you. We just got a contract to do a diving study for the Royal Saudi Navy. It won't take but six months."

I said, "Norm, I don't think I want to do it." I was thinking about the fact that my wife was getting transferred to Pax River, Maryland.

He said, "Well, what would it take you? How many dollars could we pay you to do this study?"

So I told him what it would take. He said, "Well, let me go see the president." Bob Jones was the president of QED. So they came back and said, "We can't pay you that." He said, "We can pay you this figure."

---

[*] Captain Norman E. Chalmers, USN (Ret.)
[†] The name of the company came from the Latin phrase "quod erat demonstrandum," thus it has been proven.

So I thought about it. I said, "I'll tell you what. I'll do that for you for six months." And my desk was sitting beside a retired commander, and I was making about $5,000 more a year than that retired commander. [Laughter]

So I conducted a $6 million diver study for the Royal Saudi Navy; there was $12 million in two sites. They just wanted to do one site and tailor the other site for Jubail and Jidda. I did a $12 million diver study. When I got the diver study completed, OP-40-something in Washington, D.C., approved it. Then they asked me if I would like to go to Saudi Arabia and implement it. I said, "No way! No way!" But when I got the study completed, they were building two ships in Sturgeon Bay, Wisconsin, two PGGs for the Royal Saudi Navy.*

So they asked me, "Would you stay here and do the countermeasure washdown system for those ships?"

I said, "Yeah, I'll stay."

So now I was driving from QED to Maryland on weekends because my wife was up there, and I was living in an apartment here. So I stayed and did a countermeasure washdown system.

Well, sitting at that desk, Stillwell, I think did something to my back. I went to the hospital in 1980 with back problems and got a myelogram; the disks were just floating out. They had to operate on my back, so that put me in the hospital for a little while. So they operated on my back like on a Monday. I asked the doctor, "Now, can I leave here Friday?"

He said, "You are out of your mind!"

I said, "I've got to leave out of here Friday."

He said, "What's wrong with you? You've had a major surgery!"

I said, "I've got to leave Friday."

So Thursday I got up out of bed and went to the head. The doctor said, "What's wrong with you? You can't do that."

---

* All told, Peterson Builders of Sturgeon Bay, Wisconsin, built nine guided missile patrol boats for the Saudi Navy. The first was laid down in September 1978; the last was completed in December 1982.

I said, "Yes, I can." So I went to the head.

The orthopedic surgeon of the naval hospital, Reinert, was a lieutenant commander or a commander, and he came through the ward.[*] He said, "Master Chief, can you pick up a piece of paper off the floor?"

I said, "Why, yes, sir!" And I picked up the piece of paper.

He said, "You're a damn animal. You can go if you want to." Stillwell, I was gone.

The doctor told me, "You won't be able to jog. You won't be able to lift weights. You won't be able to do it."

I said, "You fixed me, didn't you, Doc?"

He said, "Yeah, I fixed you."

I said, "Well, I'll do the rest."

And I've been doing that. I just talked to Captain Reinert the other day. He's the commanding officer over there now. You ask him about me. I left out of the hospital, but I didn't come back to work. See, I came back to my apartment and stayed two weeks and then went back to work at QED. During the two-week period I was at home, Chalmers called me and asked me, "Do you want to go to Maryland?"

I said, "Norm, I can't drive my car. I can't get out of my apartment. I'm going to do what the doctor said."

He said, "I didn't ask you that. Do you want to go to Maryland?"

I said, "You're doggone right!"

QED had an airplane, two of them. They came to my house and got me, helped me down those steps, put me in that airplane, flew me to Pax River. [Laughter] And then said, "Call me up when you want to come back." So I just laid in bed up there for four or five days, I called up, and they sent the plane back and got me. So I came back and went to work. I got the countermeasure washdown system completed on the PGGs for the Royal Saudi Navy.[†]

---

[*] Commander Charles M. Reinert, MC, USNR.
[†] The PCGs are four guided missile corvettes built for the Saudi Navy by Tacoma Boatbuilding, Tacoma, Washington, Between May 1979 and January 1983.

At that time the Forrestal was down in Florida going through the first steps of the SLEP program. So he said, "If we give you a certain amount of dollars, will you go down there and do the electronics dry air system, the LP air system, and the HP air system for the SLEP program?"[*]

I said, "Well, I guess I will."

Hattie was getting mad then, see. She was up in Maryland. So I went to Florida, and I did the SLEP inspection on the electronics dry air system and HP and LP air systems. So now I'd been with QED for about 18 months.

Q: What was involved in those things on the Forrestal?

Master Chief Brashear: Well, we were inspecting it to send her to Philadelphia for the SLEP program. My job was to go to the compressor. See, I was going to do the HP air system or the flask, and then I would inspect each foot of that pipe, Grove reducers, oil separators, unions, valves, throughout that system, same as the electronic dry air system. I would inspect it from the engine room all the way to the bridge and document on a 2 Kilo what I found.[†] Some of the piping system you would find 3,000-PSI pipes, but you might have a 1,500-PSI valve in it--things of this nature.[‡]

Q: It sounds as if you had to do a very thorough job.

Master Chief Brashear: Very thorough job by looking at a print or drawing and then chasing this pipe throughout that aircraft carrier, down compartments, up, down, a lot of ladder climbing. You could do it any way you wanted to, but we had a deadline to meet. So, being down in Florida with no air-conditioning on the ship, I used to go to the ship about 6:00 o'clock in the morning. I would get enough inspecting done to write 2 Kilos back in my hotel room till 6:00 or 7:00 o'clock at night.

---

[*] LP--low pressure; HP--high pressure.
[†] The 2K is a standard Navy form.
[‡] PSI--pounds per square inch.

Q: That's a full day.

Master Chief Brashear: Oh, yes. Yes, we were getting overtime. We made good money. I was making a lot of money. So I did that, came back to Virginia, and then I said, "Norm, I've got to quit." So I quit and went to Maryland and went to college for the next two years.

Q: What did you get your degree in?

Master Chief Brashear: I didn't. I got right up to graduating in environmental science and didn't finish.

Q: Why not?

Master Chief Brashear: She went to Puerto Rico. By that time, we were having trouble. I came to Norfolk. In Maryland I would have gotten my associate degree in 80-some hours. But when I transferred my credits down to here, they didn't honor some credits. So I was going to have to go longer, and I just got hardheaded. I said, "Well, I won't go at all. I'll quit."

Then I went to work for CDI Marine in selective records. My job there was updating ship's information books, books of general plans. In the meantime, I put in my application to the area personnel to be evaluated as an engineer and technician, and it was approved with GS-5 through GS-9. So they put me on the federal register. Well, I'd been at CDI Marine about eight months until they needed someone for a job here at CAMSLant.[*] The department head had heard about me--that's what he told me on the phone--so he seemed to think that I was the guy to kick this thing off.

---

[*] CAMS Lant--Communication Area Master Station Atlantic.

Here at CAMSLant they had this position because the environmental program and the energy program had gotten too big for LantDiv to take care of it as a collateral type of duty.* Paul Rutkowsky, an environmental engineer, was doing CAMSLant environmental work. So they created this position here and brought me into here as a GS-5.

When Mr. Molineaux called me up, I said, "I'm not going to quit my $20,000-some a year job to come to you as a GS-5."† And at that time, though, CDI Marine was losing contracts left and right. I said to myself, "Now, I could be lost, too, in these contracts. I think I'll go there as a GS-5 and make it work." So I started here in November of '82 as a GS-5, and the job has gotten so big till it's qualified for a GS-11. That's what I am now.

Q: Could you talk some about the work you've done here, please?

Master Chief Brashear: Yes. I have done a tremendous amount of work here for CAMSLant. My title is environmental protection specialist and energy conservation specialist. I think since I've been here I've reduced the energy consumption here by 30%, not only here but in my component activities at Sugar Grove, West Virginia, Annapolis, Maryland, and Driver, Virginia.

Q: How did you go about doing that?

Master Chief Brashear: By good energy management without using dollars. Now, that means that watching the systems, keeping the boilers working at 85% to a 90% of capacity--and that's good for a boiler--turning out unnecessary lights, turning off unnecessary equipment. Just good energy management without any capital investment is my procedure. I go out and talk and show slides and talk energy.

Since I've been here, I have never had to spend dollars on an ETAP project, which is an energy technology application program. Yet we've reduced energy by 30%--40% in Sugar

---

* LantDiv--the Atlantic Division of the Naval Facilities Engineering Command.
† Lieutenant Commander Ian Molineaux, USN (Ret.), public works department.

Grove--just by good management. I don't talk BTUs when I go out to give my briefs.[*] I talk dollars. Because you can talk BTUs all day and people don't know what you're talking about. But you start mentioning dollars, and then you'll raise some eyebrows. I emphasize how we can take these dollars and spend them somewhere else.

As far as the environmental side of the house, I'm PCB-free at Driver, Virginia. I've got contracts and got them funded, no PCBs at Driver. In Annapolis, Maryland, I have four PCB transformers left, but those transformers are well in compliance with the Environmental Protection Agency, because I've gone out and conducted my own dielectric strength test, analyzed my samples. I'm well in compliance with the exception of the concrete itself, and I'll never get in compliance with that. Sugar Grove, West Virginia, I'm well in compliance with the EPA. Our underground storage tanks are on track to be updated, taken out of the ground, or properly abandoned in place.

My major claimant is TelCom in Washington, D.C., and from the $140,000 I saved TelCom last year, I got another cash award, by the major claimant. Every time someone goes up there, they will say how good our programs are in energy and environmental.

Q: It sounds like the studying that you did at college in Maryland paid off even if you didn't get the degree, because you've obviously put that to use.

Master Chief Brashear: Yes. I have put it to very good use. I'm the liaison between NavCAMSLant, the Naval Environmental Support Activity in Port Hueneme, California, the Chesapeake Division of the Naval Facilities Engineering Command in Washington, and the Atlantic Division of Naval Facilities Engineering Command. I'm the liaison for energy and environmental issues.

Well, I can honestly say that I've been in the field and accomplished different tasks that a lot of the four-year engineers haven't accomplished, because I went out and did it. You take the dielectric strength test. As soon as I found out that they had an electrical fire over

---

[*] BTUs--British thermal units.

here in one of the buildings, that means the whole building is going to have to be demolished. Have you heard about that?

Q: No.

Master Chief Brashear: We had a PCB fire over there in a building, and we haven't proved yet when those transformers were tested. So from that lesson learned, I went out and initiated my own--I did it myself--my own ass, and conducted a dielectric strength test on all of my transformers; only one failed. So I've got a good track record here of getting things accomplished, making things happen.

Q: What are the subordinate facilities that you talked about? Could you describe those? You said Sugar Grove and Driver and Annapolis. What do they do at those facilities?

Master Chief Brashear: Sugar Grove and Annapolis are our tenants. It's unusual to have a tenant with a different geographical location, but we do it.

Q: What sort of work do these stations do?

Master Chief Brashear: There's a naval radio transmitting facility at Annapolis. They provide high- and low-frequency communications for the fleet. They are transmitters. Sugar Grove is a receiving site. And each one of the activities has military and civilians. I have a public works department at Sugar Grove and one in Annapolis, and they perform public works functions, maintenance, upkeep, PMS, and what have you.*

Q: Now, what does the one in Driver do?

---

* PMS--planned maintenance system.

Master Chief Brashear: It's a transmitting facility also. And it's government-owned, contract-operated--a GOCO outfit--and there I don't have a public works department. I have two contract administrators and one QA man.* See, the public works center here maintains us within a 50-mile radius.

Q: What sort of plans do you have for the future, Master Chief?

Master Chief Brashear: Well, my plan for the future is quit working here maybe the end of this year and go back to one of the engineering firms and get a part-time job. My goal is to get up and be happy every morning. That's my plan for the future.

Q: I suppose that's everybody's goal.

Master Chief Brashear: Yes, yes.

Q: Why are you leaving here?

Master Chief Brashear: Well, there's a time you have to step down, I think, and I promised myself when I turned 60 that I would go out and get a part-time job and try to live the rest of my life on my retirement pay. Now, that was my plan. I'll say this year I had in mind to go home until we got some projects in the mill that they asked me to stay and see them through, and since CAMSLant had been so good to me, I agreed to stay.

Q: Any overall thoughts to sum up on your Navy career and your life as a whole? We've talked about a lot.

Master Chief Brashear: Well, to sum it up, I can honestly say that I reached my goal in the Navy. It was an exciting career, it was a rewarding career, but then it wasn't a bed of roses

---

* QA--quality assurance.

either or whatever you say. I had my ups and downs in the Navy, but I would do it over if I could. I enjoyed the excitement of being a deep-sea diver. I grew a lot in the Navy. As a matter of fact, I grew up in the Navy as far as my professional life goes. I fouled up my personal life by drinking. My first wife was a good lady, but after 21 years I fouled that up. And I just enjoyed the Navy. I really did. I don't think I could have made it in civilian life with the limited education I had and my attitude. I think the Navy was the best place for me to grow up and find myself.

I came here to CAMSLant with the old "can-do" spirit. I was told when I reported in here that this job would never be anything but a GS-7. I said, "Well, we'll see." So I initiated things, initiated programs, wrote my own PD on several occasions to let the people know what I do, because they're not going to come out and dig in.[*] You've got to tell people what you do and what you accomplish. Some people say it's blowing your own whistle, but you've got to let people know what you do. And CCPO graded it to a GS-11, most likely could get a 12 if I stayed here.[†] And I've enjoyed it. I've learned a lot. I feel comfortable being in workshops with the professional engineers. I feel comfortable talking to senators, congressmen, admirals, captains on the environmental program. I've had the occasion to meet, correspond with congressmen, senators concerning SARA--the Superfund Amendment and Reauthorization Act. I've set up workshops with them, briefed them. I've learned a lot here. And a lot of this stuff I'm doing now was foreign to me when I started here. But I set myself up a good library, and I know where to find it, and I make it work.

Q: What sort of progress have you seen in racial relations in your lifetime and in your career in the Navy?

Master Chief Brashear: Well, I saw a lot of racial tension in my early stages of the Navy as far as down in Key West, Florida. When I first went there, blacks could only go swimming on Saturday mornings from 10:00 to 12:00 in the swimming pool. You had certain places

---

[*] PD--position description.
[†] CCPO--consolidated civilian personnel office.

you could sit in the movie. That created a lot of tension. Aboard ships I have actually seen a couple of different standards for blacks compared to whites. That created a lot tension, a lot of hate, a lot of discontent. And a lot of promotions and, you know, people think this couldn't be done, but there's a way you could do this. I've seen a lot of people promoted and left blacks by the wayside just on how you document their quarterly marks, what kind of writeup you give them. This will create a lot of tension.

I believe now that we've got programs for opportunity. People may not like you--they may hate your guts--but I don't think they can keep you down if you qualify and you have a desire to excel. Now, I'm going to use myself as an example. When I was on the Opportune, it was the first diving ship I went aboard. The boatswain on that ship told me he didn't like me because I was colored. But that didn't bother me. See, I didn't retaliate in not doing my job or trying to shirk my duty. He didn't like me. I wasn't working only for him. I was working for the captain, the United States Navy, and working for myself.

After a while, I had the highest quarterly marks of any boatswain's mate on the ship. He would invite people over to his house, but he wouldn't invite me. But I didn't let it bother me like some of the kids did in the Navy. I used to see guys in the Navy, blacks in particular--if they thought they were getting mistreated, they wouldn't want to work. I used to try to tell them, "You're not hurting them. You're hurting yourself." So I never developed that attitude, but I've seen a lot of tension build up, a lot of hate just by things like this going on.

Q: Do you think that true equal opportunity does exist in the Navy now?

Master Chief Brashear: No, it doesn't. We've made a lot of progress, but it's not equal yet. There are some areas that we're lacking. For instance, look at the admirals. See, we've got a whole bunch of white admirals, but we don't have that many blacks. And we've got some blacks that I met when I was with Hattie that I just don't know. Well, now, a couple of them kept themselves down, because they didn't want to get out and take the responsibility of having a command. They wanted to stay at these universities. But, in my opinion, there is something lacking as far as equality in that area. In the lower ranks, I believe that we are equal. But I don't believe we are in flag ranks and in the upper echelon.

Q: Certainly not on a percentage basis.

Master Chief Brashear: No. No, we're not.

Q: What would you say about attitudes now?

Master Chief Brashear: Attitudes have improved a lot, and I found that the overall attitude is a lot different from what it used to be.

Q: Well, you yourself are an example of somebody who's judged on the quality of his work, and obviously you've been judged as a success time after time.

Master Chief Brashear: Yes, but I just have a different attitude. I used to see people having bad attitudes, particularly blacks. When I go out and talk, I tell it like it is in the speeches I give. They just have a bad attitude too. Knowing that it was there, they would retaliate in the wrong way. You know, instead of proving to this guy that, "Hey, I can work with you whether you like me or not. I'm just here to do my job." And that was my attitude.

I recall--oh, my God!--they picked on me terrible when I moved from the steward branch into the deck force on the USS Palau in 1951. The first class had me running around the ship looking for a bucket of steam, you know. Now, I could have taken that as racial.

Q: I don't think that's a racial thing.

Master Chief Brashear: I don't either, but a lot of people would. This is the way I took it. We may have this on the tape. I was a third class petty officer, and he was a first class.

Twelve years later--see, I tell this story often--12 years later I saw this same man. He was a first class boatswain's mate and I was a chief. And I thought, "Now, if he would have been teaching this old farm boy what I was supposed to know, maybe he would have been a chief." That's the way I took it.

Q: Well, we're right near the end of the tape. Any final thoughts?

Master Chief Brashear: Well, enjoyed you coming down and spending the time with me. Looking forward to the result.

Q: I have a great deal of admiration for you, Master Chief, and all that you've accomplished. It's been both an honor and a privilege to hear your story.

Master Chief Brashear: Well, as I say, I'm pleased with my success and my accomplishments. A lot of people say I pat myself on the back, but I can't offend anybody when I'm talking about myself. I've reached my goal. My background and my education, I think I was very successful in the Navy, and I think I've been successful here at CAMSLant.

Q: Well, thank you for doing a successful oral history and leaving that as a legacy for future historians to work with.

Master Chief Brashear: Thank you.

Index To

Reminiscences of

Master Chief Boatswain's Mate Carl M. Brashear

U.S. Navy (Retired)

AD Skyraider
These Douglas-built planes were involved in a number of crashes at the Quonset Point Naval Air Station in the late 1950s, 50

Accidents
Brashear lost his leg during an attempt in March 1966 to rescue a nuclear bomb lost into the sea off Palomares, Spain, 81-83; role of the Naval Safety Center in the mid-1970s in monitoring and correcting safety problems, 139-145

Air Force, U.S.
Lost a nuclear weapon in water off Spain in January 1966 when two aircraft collided, 81-83; the hospital at Torrejon Air Force Base in Spain treated Brashear's injured leg in March 1966, 84-85

Albany, USS (CG-10)
Cruiser that provided short-term medical treatment when Brashear's leg was injured during a salvage incident off Spain in March 1966, 83-84

Alcohol
Brashear dealt with his problem of alcoholism in the late 1970s through the Navy's rehabilitation program, 146-151

Ammunition
Recovery of 3-inch/50 ammunition lost by the aircraft carrier Bennington (CVS-20) off Brooklyn, New York, in 1954, 34-36

Argentia, Newfoundland
Site of a Navy salvage of a merchant ship in the 1950s, 41-43

Arizona, USS (BB-39)
Brashear dove on the wreck of this ship in Pearl Harbor in the early 1960s, 63-65

Army, U.S.
Aggressive recruiting tactics drove Brashear away in 1948, 8-9

Axtell, Chief Ship Repair Technician Clair F., Jr., USN
In the mid-1960s helped Brashear get back into diving after a severe leg injury, 87-89

B-52 Stratofortress
Lost a nuclear bomb into the sea off Spain in January 1966 when it collided with a tanker aircraft, 81-83

Bayonne, New Jersey
Site of salvage diving school in the mid-1950s, 23-33; unpleasant living conditions for divers going through training, 33

Bends
　　Decompression is necessary for divers returning to the surface of the water, in order to prevent the bends, 27-28

Bennington, USS (CVS-20)
　　Recovery of 3-inch/50 ammunition lost by this ship off Brooklyn, New York, in 1954, 34-36

Blue Angels
　　Navy flight demonstration team that performed at the September 1968 commissioning of the aircraft carrier John F. Kennedy (CVA-67) at Newport News, Virginia, 101-102

Bonham, Lieutenant Commander Charlie L., USN
　　Former enlisted man who commanded the salvage ship Opportune (ARS-41) in the mid-1950s, 47

Bonin Islands
　　Installation of a mooring buoy at Chichi Jima in the late 1950s, 59-62

Boxing
　　Ship's boxing team on board the escort carrier Tripoli (CVE-64) in the early 1950s, 18-19

Brashear, Master Chief Boatswain's Mate Carl M., USN (Ret.)
　　Boyhood in Kentucky in the 1930s and 1940s, 1-7; education of, 1-2, 4, 7-8, 19-20; parents of, 1-6, 8; siblings of, 2-3; personality included a love for exciting, daring things, 5-6; enlisted in the Navy in 1948, 8-9; recruit training at Great Lakes, Illinois, in 1948, 9-11; assigned to squadron VX-1 in the late 1940s, 11-15; duty in the escort carrier Palau (CVE-122) in 1950-51, 15-17; duty in the escort carrier Tripoli (CVE-64), 1951-55, 16-22; diving school in the mid-1950s, 23-33; recovery of ammunition lost by the aircraft carrier Bennington (CVS-20) off Brooklyn, New York, in 1954, 34-36; married 1952-78 to the former Junetta Wilcoxson, 36-37, 49; duty in 1955-56 in the salvage ship Opportune (ARS-41), 37-49, 162; duty from 1956 to 1958 at Quonset Point Naval Air Station, 49-54; children of, 53, 57, 146; served 1958-60 at the ship repair facility in Guam, 54-62; in 1960 failed first-class divers school in Washington, D.C., 62; served 1961-62 at the Fleet Training Center, Pearl Harbor, 62-65; support work in 1962 for nuclear weapons testing in the Pacific by Joint Task Force Eight, 65-71; service in 1962-63 in the submarine rescue ship Coucal (ASR-8), 71-75, 79-80; in 1963-64 trained to qualify as a first-class diver, 75-79; in 1966 lost a leg during an accident on board the salvage ship Hoist (ARS-40), 81-83; service in 1968-69 in the boat house of the Norfolk Naval Air Station, 92-102; in 1969-70 attended saturation diving school at the Experimental Diving Unit in Washington, D.C., 102-110; underwent evaluation that resulted in being designated a master diver in June 1970, 110-120; served 1970-71 in the submarine tender Hunley (AS-31), 120-127; served from 1971 to 1975 in the salvage ship Recovery (ARS-43), 127-139; duty in 1975-77 at the Naval Safety Center in Norfolk, 139-145; was married from 1980 to 1983 to Navy nurse Hattie Elam, 146-147, 152, 155-156; dealt with his problem of

alcoholism in the late 1970s through the Navy's rehabilitation program, 146-151; retirement from active duty in 1979, 151-152; post-retirement employment, 152-161

Bureau of Medicine and Surgery
Review of Brashear's case after his leg was badly injured in a 1966 salvage accident, 88-91

Cabildo, USS (LSD-16)
Dock landing ship that was involved in 1962 in supporting nuclear weapons tests conducted in the Pacific by Joint Task Force Eight, 67-68

Canada
U.S. Navy salvage of a merchant ship at Argentia, Newfoundland, in the mid-1950s, 41-43; salvage of a merchant ship anchor at Labrador in the 1950s, 43-44

Chalmers, Captain Norman E., USN (Ret.)
Hired Brashear in 1979 to work for QED Corporation, 152-154, 156

Charleston Naval Shipyard, Charleston, South Carolina
Nuclear-powered submarines were serviced at Charleston in the early 1970s by the tender Hunley (AS-31), 120-127

Chichi Jima, Bonin Islands
Installation of a mooring buoy in the late 1950s, 59-62

Christmas Island
In 1962 served as the site for nuclear weapons testing by Joint Task Force Eight, 65-71

Communication Area Master Station Atlantic, Norfolk, Virginia
While working at the station in the 1980s, Brashear dealt with environmental issues, 156-161

Copenhagen, Denmark
Appealing liberty port for Navy men in the early 1950s, 17-18

Coucal, USS (ASR-8)
Submarine rescue ship that was involved in training exercises in the Pacific in the early 1960s, 71-75; divers replaced a propeller, 79-80

Delanoy, Lieutenant (junior grade) Billie L., USN
As officer in charge of the diving school in Hawaii in the early 1960s, got Brashear requalified as a second-class diver, 63

Denmark
Copenhagen was an appealing liberty port for Navy men in the early 1950s, 17-18

Discipline
Brashear was punished for stealing at pie while in recruit training at Great Lakes, Illinois, in 1948, 10; in 1962 a Navy engineman was punished for trying to break into secure spaces housing a Thor missile during nuclear weapons tests in the Pacific, 66-67

Diving
Salvage job at Key West, Florida, in the late 1940s inspired Brashear to become a diver, 16; Brashear went through salvage diving school at Bayonne, New Jersey, in the mid-1950s, 23-33; recovery of ammunition lost by the aircraft carrier Bennington (CVS-20) off Brooklyn, New York, in 1954, 34-36; involved in the salvage of a merchant ship at Argentia, Newfoundland, in the mid-1950s, 42; salvage job at Labrador in the 1950s, 43-44; procedures involved in tending a diver, 44-45; sport diving in Guam in the late 1950s, 55; scuba gear was introduced in the late 1950s, 55-57; construction of an LST ramp at Truk in the late 1950s, 58; installation of a mooring buoy at Chichi Jima in the Bonin Islands in the late 1950s, 59-62; Brashear failed first-class diver school in 1960 and had to requalify subsequently as a second-class diver, 62-63; in the early 1960s Brashear dived on the wreck of the battleship Arizona (BB-39) at Pearl Harbor, 63-65; Brashear's return to active diving after a severe leg injury in 1966, 87-91; in the late 1960s Brashear used scuba gear for work on the underwater hull of the carrier Forrestal (CVA-59), 93-94; in 1969-70 Brashear attended saturation diving school at the Experimental Diving Unit in Washington, D.C., 102-110; in June 1970 Brashear successfully completed evaluation and was designated the Navy's first black master diver, 110-120; divers from the tender Hunley (AS-31) worked on nuclear submarines at Charleston, South Carolina, in the early 1970s; in the early 1970s divers from the salvage ship Recovery (ARS-43) surveyed the merchant ship Monarch that had sunk off Newport News, Virginia, many years earlier, 127-128; divers from the Recovery went into a flooded engine room in the aircraft carrier Saratoga (CVA-60) in August 1971, 138-139; monitoring of safety-related items in the mid-1970s, 140-145

Duell, Chief Warrant Officer Raymond K., USN
In the mid-1960s helped Brashear get back into active diving after he had suffered a severe leg injury, 90-91

Dunn, Rear Admiral Robert F., USN (USNA, 1951)
Role as commander of the Naval Safety Center in 1976-77, 139-140

Education
Brashear's experiences in a segregated one-room school in Kentucky in the 1930s and 1940s, 1-2, 4, 7-8; Brashear took USAFI correspondence courses in the early 1950s, 19-20

Eisenhower, Dwight D.
Brashear went on temporary additional duty in the late 1950s to escort one of President Eisenhower's boats near Newport, Rhode Island, 50-53

Elam, Captain Hattie R., NC, USN
Was married to Brashear from 1980 to 1983, 146-147, 152, 155-156

Environmental Concerns
Studied by Brashear when he worked for the Communication Area Master Station Atlantic at Norfolk in the 1980s, 156-160

Experimental Diving Unit, Washington, D.C.
In 1969-70 Brashear attended saturation diving school and participated in a number of tests under simulated depth pressure, D.C., 102-110; in June 1970 Brashear successfully completed evaluation and was designated the Navy's first black master diver, 110-120

Experimental Squadron One (VX-1)
Operated seaplanes at Key West, Florida, in the late 1940s, 11-15

Explosives
Use of in salvage diving school at Bayonne, New Jersey, in the mid-1950s, 24, 30; use of for blasting a channel at Merizo, Guam, in the late 1950s, 54-55

Farming
Sharecropping in Kentucky in the 1930s and 1940s, 1-5

Food
Was plentiful for the sharecropping Brashear family in Kentucky in the 1930s, 2; Brashear stole a pie while in recruit training in 1948, 10

Forrestal, USS (CVA-59)
Brashear used scuba gear in the late 1960s for work on the underwater hull of the carrier while in the Norfolk Naval Shipyard, 93-94; underwent a service life extension program in the early 1980s, 155

Great Lakes (Illinois) Naval Training Station
Site of recruit training in 1948, 9-11

Guam, Marianas Islands
Use of explosives or blasting a channel at Merizo, Guam, in the late 1950s, 54-55; sport diving in the late 1950s, 55; living conditions for Navy families, 57

Guest, Rear Admiral William S., USN (USNA, 1936)
Commanded a task force that salvaged a nuclear bomb that an Air Force plane lost off Spain in 1966, 81-83

Hagerty, James
Presidential press secretary who rode an escorting crash boat when President Dwight Eisenhower was visiting Newport, Rhode Island, in the late 1950s, 50-53

Hoist, USS (ARS-40)
Salvage ship on which Brashear lost a leg in an accident while trying to recover a nuclear bomb off Spain in early 1966, 81-84

Hunley, USS (AS-31)
Provided services to nuclear submarines at Charleston, South Carolina, in the early 1970s, 120-127

John F. Kennedy, USS (CVA-67)
The Blue Angels flight demonstration team performed at the ship's commissioning in September 1967 at Newport News, Virginia, 101-102

Johnson, Master Chief Boatswain's Mate Guy P., USN (Ret.)
Arranged for Brashear to leave the steward branch while serving at Key West, Florida, in 1948, 11-12; served as a "sea daddy," 14-15

Johnston Island
In 1962 served as the site for nuclear weapons testing by Joint Task Force Eight, 65-71

Joint Task Force Eight
In 1962 conducted tests of nuclear weapons on Johnston Island and Christmas Island in the Pacific, 65-71

Key West, Florida
Base for Experimental Squadron One (VX-1) in 1948, 11-14; racial segregation for Navy men on liberty, 11, 13

Leave and Liberty
Racial segregation for Navy men on liberty in Key West, Florida, in the late 1940s, 13; Copenhagen, Denmark, was an appealing liberty port for Navy men in the early 1950s, 17-18

L. Y. Spear, USS (AS-36)
One of the ship's divers experienced a problem in the mid-1970s because of the mechanical failure of his equipment, 142

Medical Problems
In 1966 Brashear lost a leg as a result of an accident on board the salvage ship Hoist (ARS-40) and then faced a difficult recovery and rehabilitation program, 81-91; Brashear dealt with his problem of alcoholism in the late 1970s through the Navy's rehabilitation program, 146-151; Brashear was operated on for back problems in the early 1980s, 153-154

Merchant Ships
U.S. Navy salvage of a commercial ship at Argentia, Newfoundland, in the mid-1950s, 41-43

Military Sea Transportation Service
　　The escort carrier Tripoli (CVE-64) served as an aircraft ferry for MSTS in the early 1950s, 21-22

Missiles
　　Nuclear weapons tests in 1962 using the Thor missile in the Pacific, 66

Movies
　　In the mid-1970s Brashear was involved in a short documentary film called "Come Back" related to his diving experiences after losing a leg, 143

Mustin, Rear Admiral Lloyd C., USN (USNA, 1932)
　　Involved in 1962 in nuclear weapons testing in the Pacific by Joint Task Force Eight, 70-71

Naval Safety Center, Norfolk, Virginia
　　Determined in the mid-1970s that personnel errors accounted for most diving accidents, 45-46; role in the mid-1970s in monitoring and correcting safety problems, 139-145

Newport, Rhode Island
　　Brashear went on temporary additional duty in the late 1950s to escort one of President Dwight Eisenhower's boats near Newport, 50-53

Newport News Shipbuilding, Newport News, Virginia
　　The Navy's Blue Angels flight demonstration team performed at the September 1968 commissioning of the aircraft carrier John F. Kennedy (CVA-67), 101-102

Norfolk Naval Air Station
　　Role of the boat house crew in the late 1960s in salvaging downed aircraft that had gone into the water, 92-102

Norfolk Naval Hospital, Portsmouth, Virginia
　　Role in treating Brashear's injured leg in 1966, 86-89

Norfolk Naval Shipyard, Portsmouth, Virginia
　　Brashear used scuba gear for work in the late 1960s on the underwater hull of the aircraft carrier Forrestal (CVA-59), 93-94

Nuclear Propulsion
　　Nuclear-powered submarines were serviced at Charleston, South Carolina, in the early 1970s by the tender Hunley (AS-31), 120-127

Nuclear Weapons
　　In 1962 Joint Task Force Eight conducted atmospheric tests at Johnston Island and Christmas Island in the Pacific, 65-71; recovery of a nuclear bomb dropped off Spain in January 1966 in a collision of two Air Forces planes, 81-83

Opportune, USS (ARS-41)
   Various operations for this salvage ship in the mid-1950s, 37-48; had mustang officers in the mid-1950s, 47; racial climate of the crew in the 1950s, 162

PBM Mariner
   Martin-built patrol bomber operated by Squadron VX-1 at Key West, Florida, in the late 1940s, 11-14

Palau, USS (CVE-122)
   Escort aircraft carrier that operated in the Atlantic in the early 1950s, 15-17

Palomares, Spain
   Site of salvage efforts for a nuclear bomb dropped during the collision of two Air Force planes in January 1966, 81-83

Pay and Allowances
   Navy divers receive additional pay for hazardous duty, 46, 48-49

Quonset Point (Rhode Island) Naval Air Station
   Role of boat house personnel in recovering downed airplanes and aviators in the late 1950s, 49-50; Brashear went on temporary additional duty in the late 1950s to escort one of President Dwight Eisenhower's boats near Newport, 50-53

Racial Discrimination
   In Kentucky in the 1930s and 1940s, 4; at Key West, Florida, in the late 1940s, 161-162

Racial Integration
   Blacks and whites helped each other with farming in Kentucky in the 1930s and 1940s, 5; in recruit training at Great Lakes, Illinois, in 1948, 11; opportunties have improved considerably for blacks in the Navy, but equal opportunity still does not exist, 162-163

Racial Prejudice
   Brashear encountered a negative reaction when he reported for salvage diving school in the mid-1950s, 23

Racial Segregation
   Brashear's experiences in a one-room school in Kentucky in the 1930s and 1940s, 1-2, 4; for black Navy men at Key West, Florida, in 1948, 11, 13

Recruiting
   A pleasant recruiter in Elizabethtown persuaded Brashear to enlist in the Navy in 1948, 8-9

Recruit Training
   At Great Lakes, Illinois, in the winter of 1948, 9-11

Religion
Role in the Brashear family in Kentucky in the 1930s and 1940s, 3-4

Recovery, USS (ARS-43)
In the early 1970s sent divers down to inspect the merchant ship Monarch that had been sunk off Newport News, Virginia, many years earlier, 127-128; salvage of a helicopter in the early 1970s off Jacksonville, Florida, 128-129; atmosphere in the ship's chief petty officer quarters in the early 1970s, 129-130; Brashear's interaction with the crew in his role as command master chief, 130-135; had a number of mustang officers, 136; methods in preparing for diving jobs, 137; sent a team of divers to the carrier Saratoga (CVA-60) in 1971 when she had a flooded engine room, 138-139

Robinson, Sugar Ray
Black boxer who fought around New York City in the 1940s and 1950s, 18

Rutherford, Lieutenant Harry M., USN
As a boatswain's mate first class in the mid-1950s, gave Brashear needed encouragement about staying in salvage diving school at Bayonne, New Jersey, 23-24; served as executive officer of a salvage ship in Hawaii in the early 1960s, 31-32; picked Brashear for a salvage diving job off Brooklyn, New York, in 1954, 34

S2F Tracker
Mid-1950s salvage recovery of an S2F lost off the Virginia Capes, 39-40

Safety
Not particularly stressed at salvage diving school in Bayonne, New Jersey, in the mid-1950s, 30-31; sometimes disregarded during salvage jobs in the 1950s, 35-36, 39-40, 43-46; role of the Naval Safety Center in the mid-1970s in monitoring and correcting safety problems, 139-145

Salvage
A salvage job in Key West, Florida, in the late 1940s inspired Brashear to become a diver, 16; recovery of a TBM aircraft from the escort carrier Tripoli (CVE-64) in the early 1950s, recovery of ammunition lost by the aircraft carrier Bennington (CVS-20) off Brooklyn, New York, in 1954, 34-36; raising of a barge off Charleston, South Carolina, in the mid-1950s, 38; recovery of an S2F Tracker off the Virginia Capes in the mid-1950s, 39-40; of a merchant ship in Argentia, Newfoundland, in the mid-1950s, 41-43; recovery of a nuclear bomb dropped off Spain in January 1966 in a collision of two Air Forces planes, 81-83; role of the Norfolk Naval Air Station's boat house crew in the late 1960s in salvaging downed aircraft that had gone into the water, 92-102; of a helicopter off Jacksonville, Florida, in the early 1970s by the salvage ship Recovery (ARS-43), 128-129

Saratoga, USS (CVA-60)
Divers went into one of her engine rooms when it was flooded in August 1971, 138-139

Saudi Navy
Subject of a study by Brashear in the early 1980s when he worked for QED Corporation, 152-154

Scuba Diving
Self-contained underwater breathing apparatus was introduced in the late 1950s, 55-57

SEALS
A young SEAL trainee died of oxygen poisoning in the mid-1970s while swimming soon after a workout on land, 141-142

Seaplanes
Operated by Squadron VX-1 at Key West, Florida, in the late 1940s, 11-13

Spain
Palomares was the site of salvage efforts for a nuclear bomb dropped during the collision of two Air Force planes in January 1966, 81-83; Brashear's leg, badly injured during salvage efforts in March 1966, was treated at Torrejon Air Force Base in Spain, 84-85

Starbird, Major General Alfred D., USA (USMA, 1933)
Commanded Joint Task Force Eight in 1962 during nuclear weapons tests in the Pacific, 66-67

Stenke, Lieutenant George, USN
Invented the Stenke hood used for making a buoyant ascent from a submarine, 71-71, 143

Submarines
Nuclear-powered submarines were serviced at Charleston, South Carolina, in the early 1970s by the tender Hunley (AS-31), 120-127

Swimming
Brashear began to swim in Kentucky when he was a boy, 6; involved in working with seaplanes in Squadron VX-1 in Key West, Florida, in the late 1940s, 12-14; few blacks swim well because the culture does not expose them to it, 12; A young SEAL trainee died of oxygen poisoning in the mid-1970s while swimming soon after a workout on land, 141-142

Thor Missile
Used for nuclear weapons tests in 1962 in the Pacific, 66

Thurman, Commander Robert K., USN
Role in the salvage of a merchant ship at Argentia, Newfoundland, in the mid-1950s, 41-42; involved in nuclear weapons testing by Joint Task Force Eight in the Pacific in 1962, 68-69

Torrejon Air Force Base, Spain
  Brashear's injured leg was treated in the hospital at this base in March 1966, 84-85

Training
  For recruits at Great Lakes, Illinois, in 1948, 9-11; seamanship training on board the escort carrier Palau (CVE-122) in the early 1950s, 15; Brashear went through salvage diving school at Bayonne, New Jersey, in the mid-1950s, 23-33; use of the submarine rescue ship Coucal (ASR-8) to practice rescue techniques in the early 1960s, 71-73; in 1963-64 Brashear trained to qualify as a first-class diver, 75-79; in 1969-70 Brashear attended saturation diving school at the Experimental Diving Unit in Washington, D.C., 102-110

Tripoli, USS (CVE-64)
  Did a lot of operating in the early 1950s, 16-17, 21-22; loss of a TBM aircraft, 16-18; ship's boxing team, 18-19; homeported in New York in the early 1950s, 36

Truk Islands, Western Carolines
  Construction of an LST ramp in the late 1950s, 58

VX-1
  See Experimental Squadron One (VX-1)

Welding
  Techniques for welding underwater while doing salvage work, 28-29

www.ingramcontent.com/pod-product-compliance
Lightning Source LLC
Chambersburg PA
CBHW082208070526
44585CB00020B/2330